PRAISE FOR
FROM CAMDEN TO KATHMANDU

Berlin's account of his year-long odyssey as a young man offers a journey well worth following. A spiritual quest for deeper meaning, his story demonstrates how the practice of "letting go…and allowing whatever arose in the present moment" can be a guide to transforming our lives. His memoir contains many lessons we can all benefit from.

—**Henry Shukman,** author of *One Blade of Grass* and *Original Love*

Much to the dismay of his parents, 27-year-old Bruce Berlin stepped away from his nascent legal career to embark alone on a year-long spiritual "magical mystery tour" through Europe and overland to India and Nepal. Berlin was what Buddhists call a hungry ghost: someone "who could never quench his thirst or satisfy his cravings…driven by intense emotional needs…" Fifty-two years later, Berlin revisits his trip and discovers "Everything happened for a reason, though we might have no idea what that reason was." Berlin's book is the story of a meditative, and sometimes harrowing, journey on the other side of the globe, that swept me up like a hitchhiker absorbing each sound and sight for the first vivid time.

—**Albert Norman,** author of *Slam-Dunking Walmart,* and *Ravings: American Wild Talk*

A heartwarming memoir that captures the transformative spirit of the '60s and the timeless yearning of the soul to know its purpose.

—**Charlotte Levinson,** The Levinson Foundation

Berlin's memoir takes the reader on a journey, filled with adventure, that led to his finding meaning in his life and an enduring spiritual path. He captures what it is like for a young man to explore the world and his mind. His travels created the foundation for a life of purpose from which the world has greatly benefited through his work for social change. His odyssey is an inspiration to all those who are searching for their way in the world.

—**Nomi Green MA,** ordained member of the Buddhist Order of Interbeing by Zen Master Thich Nhat Hahn

This is much more than an armchair adventure read. Bruce takes us on the inner journey, where the insights come as fast and furious as the exotic locales. From the bazaars of Morocco to caves in Turkey, the Taj Mahal, the Himalayas, and beyond, his unique explorations resonate with anyone looking to illuminate their own inner path. The journey itself keeps asking, "who am I, and where am I going?" Sex, drugs and inner turmoil, set in the Vietnam war times, give way to discovering the spiritual treasures of the East. From gardens of ecstasy to dangerous crossings, the external environs mirror the questions within, the seeking for inner peace and clarity that only comes when one opens and least expects it.

—**Victor La Cerva MD,** author of *Letters To A Young Man In Search of Himself*

Bruce's story is a pithy reminder of the baby boomers' odyssey. His memoir invites us to revisit that quest for meaning and direction during those iconic years when so much was in turmoil. Take this journey with Bruce and remember, or discover, an era that was pivotal in American history.

—**The Rev. Dr. Holly Beaumont,** Organizing Director, Interfaith Worker Justice, New Mexico

Berlin leaves a predictable pathway as a young lawyer to take an epic global journey in the counter-culture of the 1970's in search of life's meaning. But his thirst is not quenched by alluring places and people throughout Europe and Asia. Rather, he discovers an inward spiritual journey which finally grounds his soul. This revealing personal account from Bruce's past offers inspiration for contemporary seekers.

—**Wesley Granberg-Michaelson,** author of *The Soul Work of Justice: Four Movements of Contemplative Action*

From Camden to Kathmandu

FROM CAMDEN TO KATHMANDU

You Don't Have to Know
Where You're Going
To Get Where You Want to Be

A MEMOIR
BRUCE BERLIN

Our Time Books
Santa Fe, New Mexico

From Camden to Kathmandu: You Don't Have to Know Where You're Going to Get Where You Want to Be

Copyright © 2025 by Bruce Berlin

No part of this book may be reproduced or transcribed in any form or by any means, mechanical or electronic, including photocopying and recording or by any information storage and retrieval system, without prior written permission from the publisher other than the inclusion of brief quotations embedded in articles and reviews.

No AI was used in writing this book.

ISBN, print: 978-0-9966232-2-3

ISBN, e-book: 978-0-9966232-3-0

LCCN: 2025914040

Our Time Books

Santa Fe, New Mexico

Editing by Melanie Mulhall, Dragonheart, www.TheDragonhheart.com and Gina Rae La Cerva

Book design by Journey Bound Publishing, www.JourneyBoundPublishing.com and Joseph Woods

First Edition

For all my teachers, especially Lama Yeshe and Thubten Zopa Rinpoche, who helped guide me on my journey and to all those around the planet who are searching for their way in the world.

CONTENTS

Introduction	1
1. Letting Go	3
2. Running to Catch My Breath	15
3. Traveling Back in Time	27
4. Gearing Up and Heading East	41
5. Looking Back and Moving Forward	51
6. Riding the Twists and Turns	61
7. Discovering a Truly Foreign Country	71
8. Hanging Out in Kabul	79
9. Arriving in India, the Promised Land	85
10. Beginning to Find Peace	93
11. Wandering in Paradise	101
12. Discovering Buddhism	109
13. Allowing the Universe to Lead the Way	113
14. Learning the Way of the Buddha	121
15. Getting on the Path to Enlightenment	135
16. Reentering the Temporal World	145
17. Making an Intimate Connection with the Buddha	155
18. Making My Way Back Home	161
Afterword	167
Photos from the Author's Journey	171
Acknowledgments	175
About the Author	177

INTRODUCTION

I AM IN A REMOTE Afghan village on market day. Hundreds of rifle-bearing men on white horses dressed in white robes and turbans surround me. Our vehicle is the only one in this tiny, nameless place in the middle of nowhere. We stopped here for lunch on the second day of a three-day trek through the high desert from Herat to Mazar-i-Shariff in northern Afghanistan. For most of the journey, we haven't even been riding on a road, just following tracks in the desert.

I'm traveling with three other Westerners jammed in the back of a vintage, open-air truck with about twenty Afghan men and their rugs and packs. I never could have imagined I'd be traveling like this when I left the States five months ago. The year is 1972, and my life is rapidly changing.

I feel like I'm on a Hollywood movie set or that I've been suddenly propelled a couple of centuries or more back in time. I'm on the other side of the globe, experiencing firsthand how different people's lives are from mine in the States. I could hardly believe we live on the same planet. While I've been to several out-of-the-way locales during my journey, this is unquestionably the most foreign place I've ever been to. And I'm having one amazing adventure after another.

I had no itinerary when I boarded a plane to Amsterdam in May. It seemed like the perfect time to take off since I didn't have a job or a place to call home. So I sold the car I'd bought mostly with money my parents had given me as a law school graduation present and made my plane reservations. Very excited and a bit apprehensive, I set off to find myself and my place in the world.

Escaping from the demands of middle-class America and jumping into the unknown magic of global exploration was a venture I couldn't resist. I never could have imagined the incredible adventures I would have or the remarkable people I would meet in my travels. It lifted my spirit and deepened my soul like nothing else ever could.

I didn't really know where I was going—either geographically or with my life—but one of the things I discovered was this: You don't have to know where you're going to get where you want to be.

1

LETTING GO

EVERYTHING WAS HAPPENING SO FAST. Friday afternoon, I was in Newark completing the New Jersey bar exam. Forty hours later, I was in the Black Hills of South Dakota tripping on LSD for the first time.

After spending six weeks studying for the bar, I was free at last and eager to begin my cross-country adventure. As soon as I finished the exam, I caught a plane to Omaha, where my cousin Eddie and two of his friends met me at the airport. Eddie and I had been close for a long time, but I barely knew his two buddies. The three of them had left Jersey a few days earlier, driving to meet me in Omaha. Together, we would continue heading west in the new Ford van we had bought for the trip.

The next day we drove to the Black Hills with Deje, a hitchhiker my traveling companions had picked up on their way to Omaha. Never considering we would have another passenger, I was somewhat surprised that they had brought him along. A quiet, mysterious guy, Deje looked worn beyond his years. I couldn't really tell how old he was, maybe forty, maybe fifty. Who knew?

Deje lived in the back woods of the Dakota hills. Wanting to see Mt. Rushmore, we decided to drive north, out of our way and take him back home. By the time we reached the Black Hills, it was pitch black out. With no moon or street lamps, we had only the van's headlights and Deje to guide us.

"I think we should turn left up here," he said without much conviction.

"Are you sure?" I asked nervously.

"Well," Deje replied hesitantly, "I've lived here a long time. This looks right." At this point, the only thing we could do was trust that he'd find the way. After a few more turns—one of which was in the wrong direction—we finally arrived at his cabin, where we all settled in for the night.

The next morning Deje and a few of his hippie pals turned us on to some acid they called "sunshine." Deje assured us it was "good shit. Nothing to worry about." Reading about Ram Dass's extensive LSD trips was fascinating, but I never imagined dropping acid myself. Then, just like that, a little yellow pill appeared in my hand that would soon turn my head around.

My body began tingling and my head was light. The brown and green colors of the hills intensified. Suddenly, the acid triggered a blast of energy to every cell in my body. I felt alive like never before.

"Wow!" I yelled. I couldn't quite grasp what was happening to me, but I liked it.

Eight of us then began climbing a small, rugged hill. It had just stopped raining, and a smoky mist covered the hills creating a stark, dreamlike atmosphere. I shivered in the cool, damp air as we ascended the hill. Deje slowly led the way. Slightly bowed due to a fused backbone, his tall, thin frame was strikingly Christ-like.

At the summit, we sat in a small circle with the morning haze hanging over us. I imagined we were at the entrance to heaven. It felt surreal. Eddie was so blown away that he couldn't contain himself. He jumped up and threw his watch into the abyss, literally letting go of time.

The intensity of the moment, along with the moist mountain air, chilled me to the bone. Deje rose to his feet holding a wooden staff in one hand. Right in front of me, I saw him transform from Christ to Moses about to deliver the Ten Commandments to us. As I was tripping out of my mind, Deje appeared to be a messenger from another dimension bringing all faiths together. His strong, gentle voice struck a deep chord. I felt his simple declaration shattered the barriers that divide humankind.

"We are all brothers and sisters here to come together as one. It is our duty and the only way forward."

Mesmerized by Deje's words and powerful presence, I was spellbound, certain that Deje had come to awaken my spirit. My awareness rose to a higher state of consciousness while my whole body vibrated in a way I had never experienced before. I felt lighter and bonded with everyone in the circle, even though I had just met them. For the first time in my life, I had tapped into the field of universal energy that interconnects all matter, bringing everything together as one. I could actually see bright flashes of light emanating to and from my body in all directions.

The little yellow sunshine pill was working its magic. I imagined some form of supernatural surgery had been performed on my mind, opening the door to another world I had no idea existed. I was discovering another layer of dynamic energy beyond what we normally observe.

A couple of hours later, as we leisurely drifted down the hill, I began to slowly come down from the LSD. By midafternoon, we were back at Deje's cabin, eating our first meal of the day. While tripping, I had more than enough energy just from the acid. By evening, I was exhausted and fell asleep as soon as my head hit the pillow.

The next morning, after profusely thanking Deje for the mystical time of my life, we hit the road again. We drove, camped, and hiked in the majestic Colorado Rockies. Being in that high country wonderland for the first time, I loved every minute of it. Two weeks later, we arrived in Las Vegas just in time to attend the midnight show of the Broadway musical *Hair* on the Vegas Strip.

Before leaving on our cross-country holiday, Eddie had obtained some recreational drugs to enrich our experience. Going to see *Hair* felt like an opportune time to get high on the mescaline he had brought with him. After our acid trip experience, I was all in.

We were seated in the third row. Having taken the mescaline just before the show, Eddie and I were soaring. When the cast belted out "The Age of Aquarius," I sensed they were echoing Deje's message of oneness. My spirit danced to the music as I wondered what it would mean if the Age of Aquarius did permeate the planet. Following the show, Eddie and I were higher than ever. No way we could sleep after that, so we stayed up all night and gazed at the intense, desert sunrise the next morning.

We couldn't leave Vegas without trying our luck at the blackjack table. While free drinks were all we won, we were wise enough to quit before our losing hands made much of a dent in our pockets. Later that day, we said goodbye to the bright lights of the Vegas Strip and took to the highway once again.

Driving from Vegas to California, the words and music from *Hair* reverberated in my head. It was as though the Age of Aquarius was coming into view just over the horizon. But it was only an alluring mirage.

Just a few short weeks later, our summer adventure ended at the San Francisco airport. From there, I flew back East to begin my career as a lawyer at the Legal Aid Society in Trenton, New Jersey.

I was quickly pulled back down to Earth as I began learning the realities of the practice of law. It wasn't what I had hoped for. Not that I expected to be like Perry Mason, trying big, complex legal cases and making eloquent closing arguments before a jury. I just wanted to feel I was making a real difference. When I prevented a poor tenant from being evicted or helped a welfare recipient maneuver through the confusing bureaucracy to receive the monthly amount to which she was entitled, I was helping people, but I never thought it was enough. Instead of dealing with the root cause of a client's ongoing predicament, I felt that I was just putting a bandage on the problem. In two or three months, that poor tenant would be behind in his rent again and receive another eviction notice, or the welfare recipient would not be getting her monthly check for one reason or another and would again need legal assistance.

My passion for making a difference wanted more. I majored in government at Cornell because I imagined myself in some government job, making a difference in people's lives as well as in larger national issues. That was also the main reason I went to law school. I had lofty aspirations. So I went to work at Legal Aid, where I thought I could help people who could not afford private counsel. But my Legal Aid job just didn't satisfy my deep hunger for meaning and making societal change. I felt more like a hamster running on a wheel, getting nowhere.

By the summer of 1971, my dissatisfaction with my Legal Aid work, as well as with living in Trenton, made my next step toward freedom easier. I felt disillusioned and wondered if the practice of law was really for me. Frustrated, I quit my job, packed up my belongings, and headed to Boston to live with my cousin Eddie, who was in his last year at Harvard Law School.

Finding any employment in the middle of the Nixon recession was no easy task. Because I was not a member of the Massachusetts Bar, I couldn't do legal work, not that I actually wanted to. After a couple of months of playing cards and taking a photography course, I began to substitute teach at an Arlington middle school to pay my living expenses. I was merely treading water. But when I started looking for a full-time job I truly wanted, I realized I had no idea what that job might be.

My whole life was thrown into question. Up to that point, everything had been neatly laid out for me. Seven years of college and law school would presumably lead to a secure career in the legal profession. Then marriage, kids, and the good life in suburbia would naturally follow. It would all be so easy. But suddenly, it wasn't.

I began to sense that there was more to life. Having purpose and passion for my work meant a lot to me—much more than just making a living as a lawyer. I could not envision work without them. My dad and I had debated this issue on several occasions while I was in high school and college.

"For ninety-nine percent of the people, that is the way life is," he said. "For the other one percent, the geniuses, it's different. Their work is filled with purpose and passion. But most of us go to work because we have to make a living to support ourselves and our families. Hobbies and avocations are what give me satisfaction and fulfillment."

"That's crazy," I replied. "No one should do work they don't enjoy."

"You'll see," he cautioned.

Still, residing in my ivory tower of higher education, I could not refute his many years of real-life experience. Dad was a dentist, the one thing I knew was not for me. I couldn't imagine standing up all day and looking in people's mouths. He told me he enjoyed it half the time. But he admitted that the other half of the time, he was doing what he had to so he could pay the rent and put food on the table for our family. Genius or not, I vowed to myself that I'd never get stuck in a boring, routine job merely to make a living.

At the same time, I had another challenge demanding my attention. In 1968, I was in law school at NYU while America's involvement in the Vietnam War continued to grow. The Military Selective Service Act of 1967 had eliminated my graduate school deferment. Like many others who feared getting shipped to Vietnam, I anxiously looked for a way out. I decided to join the Arny Reserves rather than chance being drafted. As more and more troops were needed in Vietnam, the Army started calling up reservists like me. I felt my life was at risk.

I needed to get out of the Reserves before I found myself in the jungles of Vietnam fighting a war I strongly opposed. At Cornell, I studied how the United States became embroiled in the Vietnam War. Vietnam had been a French colony since

1877. When the French were defeated by Ho Chi Minh's communist forces in 1954, the US believed it had to take up the fight to prevent the spread of communism.

Books like David Halberstam's *The Quagmire in Vietnam* convinced me that the US did not belong there. We were supporting a corrupt South Vietnamese government against Ho Chi Minh's nationalist movement, which had the backing of the majority of the Vietnamese people. The US championed the domino theory to justify its intervention in what was essentially a civil war. The Johnson administration maintained South Vietnam's falling to the communists would lead to Laos and other neighboring countries falling to the communists, one by one, like dominos in a row.

By the time I joined the Reserves, more than a half million Americans were fighting in Vietnam. Thousands were being killed in a war that was none of our business, and I wanted no part of it. When President Johnson began calling for more and more US troops to be sent to Vietnam, I took to the streets in protest with hundreds of thousands of outraged Americans.

"Hell no, we won't go! Hell no, we won't go!" I chanted along with the huge crowd as we marched past the White House on our way to the Washington Monument one bitter cold morning in mid-November 1969. As a marshal for the Vietnam War Moratorium, the national organization calling for an end to the war, I was up at 5:00 a.m. preparing to help control the angry protesters. Like many law students serving as marshals, my job was to ensure that the marchers didn't violate the rules of the moratorium, let alone break the law. The demonstration's organizers wanted to avoid violence at all costs. No one wanted to give Richard Nixon, the newly elected

Republican president, an excuse to dismiss the protest as a bunch of young hooligans.

Shivering as I stood at my assigned post, I could not believe how many people—at least a half million—had come from all over the country to deliver a message to the president. "Peace now! Peace now!" we shouted.

While the sea of people passed by, I felt a strong sense of pride in being a part of this historic event. Later that afternoon at the Washington Monument, I was deeply stirred by the speeches of anti-war movement leaders like Senator Eugene McCarthy. Tears ran down my cheeks as Peter, Paul and Mary sang, "Where Have All the Flowers Gone?" I looked to my left into the eyes of my fellow marshal, whose right arm embraced my waist. His eyes glistened with tears as well. Then I looked to my right at the stranger whose left hand grasped my shoulder. She was crying too. I couldn't remember another time in my life when I had been so moved.

Since then, my disgust for the war had only grown. When I began working for Legal Aid, I swore that there was no way I would go to Vietnam. I had to find a way out of the Reserves. I started seeing a psychiatrist in Trenton who was known to assist guys wanting to avoid serving in Vietnam. After a few months of therapy sessions, he agreed to write a letter to the Army Reserves explaining that, in his professional opinion, I was not mentally fit to serve in the military. In short order, I received my discharge from the Reserves with a 4F classification, which meant that I was deemed unfit for military service due to physical, mental, or moral reasons.

I was so relieved! I'd taken a big step toward freeing myself from an America that was becoming more and more alien to me. With Nixon in the White House, race riots in major cities over the last several years, the assassinations of Bobby Kennedy and Martin Luther King, Jr, and Kent State students being killed by the National Guard, I was extremely troubled by the horrific state of my country.

By the spring of 1972, after eight months of doing very little in Lexington, Massachusetts, I knew I had to do something. Eddie was graduating and had been offered a clerkship. And the lease was up on our rental house. The professor who owned the house was returning from his sabbatical and would be moving back in. Since I had never been to Europe and had no concrete job prospects, I decided this was the opportune time to go.

A couple of weeks later, I ran into my old college sweetheart, Frances, and her husband, Steven, in Harvard Square. I hadn't seen them in well over a year and had no idea what was happening in their lives. They told me they had just returned from a winter in India.

"What did you do there?" I asked. "I am about to travel abroad, though India has never entered my mind as a possible destination." They were in a hurry but invited me over to their place for an evening so they could tell me all about their foreign adventures. Not long after that, we got together. I turned them on to some fine weed and they turned me on to the mysteries of India.

Frances and Steven's tale was not of a beautiful, exotic land. Rather, they described the filth and poverty of an overpopulated, undereducated society run by a chaotic, self-serving bureaucracy.

"So why in the world did you go there?" I asked.

"That you must discover for yourself," Frances replied.

Something in the way she answered told me there actually was more to India than hunger and hordes of poor people.

My friends had acquired a deeper understanding that they could not, or would not, readily convey. But they piqued my curiosity. If I wanted to know more, I would have to unearth India's secrets for myself.

A few weeks later, I bid my family farewell. My mother cried as if I were going off to war and might not return. I vowed I would be back in a few months, but that didn't seem to relieve her anxiety. Her fear of the unknown moved her much more than my attempts to comfort her.

My parents were disturbed by the increasing distance, both philosophically and physically, that had come between us since I left my Legal Aid position the year before. After eight months of unemployment, I was not seeking a job as a lawyer as they had hoped. On the contrary, I was following Walt Whitman's lead from his *Song of the Open Road*:

Afoot and light-hearted I take to the open road,
Healthy, free, the world before me,
The long brown path before me leading wherever I choose.

Taking to the open road was beyond the realm of my parents' experience or comprehension. And I also had some concerns. Traveling alone was a new and somewhat daunting experience for me. I had no plan, hardly any foreign contacts, and almost no ability to communicate in any language other than English. A pack on my back and a couple of maps were my only companions when I boarded my flight to Europe. As I fastened my seatbelt and prepared for takeoff, my path and my destiny were a complete unknown, an intriguing mystery to me.

2

RUNNING TO CATCH MY BREATH

FROM THE BEGINNING OF MY journey, I found myself running around Europe practically nonstop, trying to see and do as much as possible as quickly as possible. There was so much to take in. Yet I could never quite keep pace with my desire for something more. When my experience fell short of my expectations, I quickly consulted a map and rushed off to a new destination.

Though I didn't realize it then, I was becoming what the Buddhists call a *hungry ghost*, one who could never quench his thirst or satisfy his cravings. In Buddhism, hungry ghosts are beings driven by intense emotional needs that cannot get their desires met. They're creatures with pinhole mouths and necks so tiny they cannot swallow. They can never fill their bulging, empty stomachs. Whatever they try to ingest turns to fire or ice, which can't pass through their minuscule throats to their very large bellies. In effect, I was trapped in the Hungry Ghost Realm—a realm below the Human Realm but above the Hell Realm—where I was constantly seeking something outside myself to curb an insatiable yearning deep within me. But for what, I had no clue.

I began my quest in Amsterdam. With its charming canals, remarkable history, and laid-back lifestyle, it was one of the most popular tourist destinations in Europe during the spring of 1972. I felt comfortable there, though I was alone. Many people spoke English, so that wasn't a problem. Plus, they were friendly. Maybe a little too friendly. In the red-light district scantily dressed women hung out of open windows, tempting men to come inside with them.

"Hey, come here. Don't you want to play with me?" one lady of the night coaxed seductively. Like much of her competition, she looked a little too made up and a little too worn out and unappealing. While I refused countless invitations from her and her colleagues, I did feel for these unfortunate women prostituting themselves to make a living. Seeing them plying their wares gave me a deeper appreciation for how difficult their lives were. More than that, it began my firsthand education of how impoverished much of the world's population was in numerous ways.

Still, Amsterdam had other attractions I couldn't resist, like spending a morning at the Heineken brewery. After a tour of the facilities and learning how they make their famous beer, I sat down in the tasting room with a few other brewski aficionados and drank as much as I could of their finest drafts. After forty-five minutes or so, I stumbled out of there half smashed and feeling fine. In my drunken state, my hungry ghost couldn't care less whether I had discovered any deeper meaning that morning. I was having a very good time, and that was all that mattered.

A much more sobering experience was my visit to the Anne Frank House. Being Jewish, a history buff, and knowing some bits of Anne Frank's harrowing story, I wished to learn more about her. I wanted to see the secret annex where her family hid from the Nazis for two years during World War II. Anne, her sister Margot, their parents, and four other Jews subsisted in a cramped, tiny space for two years until they were discovered in August 1944.

I was filled with tremendous sadness and anger as I saw how they lived and later died under the Nazis' horrific policy of eradicating the entire European Jewish population. During the tour of the house, I learned that Anne's father, Otto, was the only one in the family who somehow survived the death camps.

This history of inhumanity toward Jews was part of my heritage. As I toured the Franks' hideaway, I wondered why the Jews seemed to be the world's scapegoat. What did we do to deserve this? How could people brutalize other human beings with such organized cruelty? It was incomprehensible to me. Would my hungry ghost ever find relief from these burning issues?

Leaving the Anne Frank House with tears in my eyes, I screamed, trembling with rage. Deep inside, I knew that the world was not very safe for Jews, and I could suffer a similar annihilation. The world seemed shaky and dark—ripe for blaming the Jews and spreading antisemitism.

The next morning I had to do something life-affirming. And what could be more uplifting than going to see the works of some of the world's most renowned artists? I had studied the paintings of Rembrandt and Van Gogh in my college art history course. Seeing them in person gave me a sense of reverence I could never have gotten from pictures in a book. Viewing Rembrandt's immense *Night Watchman* at the Rijksmuseum and touring the Van Gogh Museum with its beautiful post-impressionist collection did provide my hungry ghost with a little gratification. But I was not satisfied and craved for more. Like all hungry ghosts, my desire was unquenchable.

So I jumped on a boat and took my longings across the English Channel to London. I had never felt so lonely as I did in London. A stranger in a huge foreign metropolis, I had no one to show me the sites or give me a helping hand. While visiting Big Ben and Buckingham Palace, I realized what I longed for was a connection with people. For my journey to have greater meaning, meeting the people of the countries I was visiting felt critical, but it was not so simple. Londoners always seemed to be in a rush or perhaps just very self-contained. And being a bit of an introvert, it was not easy for me to stop a stranger who appeared in a hurry and ask how to get somewhere.

I felt challenged and uncomfortable. There was so much I wanted to see there, but the loud, big city energy was too much for me. Making my way through the masses of people and concrete, I had a strong sense of aloneness. I needed to escape, and after a few isolated days, I did.

I left London and took to the English highways with that hungry ghost still inside me, longing for kinship. Open to wherever my journey would take me next, I decided hitch-hiking might be my entry into meeting local folks. I headed to the west end of the city, where I put my thumb out seeking a ride. A quiet, middle-aged couple, Mr. and Mrs. Thomas, soon stopped and picked me up in their tiny Austin Mini. Squeezed in the back seat with luggage piled high to my right and their frisky pup in my lap, I was glad to finally be making a real human connection with an English couple.

The Thomases drove me 237 miles, all the way to Plymouth on the southwest coast of England. They were returning home after driving their son back to university following his school vacation. As we sped through the English countryside, I barely caught a glimpse of mystical Stonehenge off in the distance. A prehistoric ring of huge standing stones, it had been high on my list of sites to see. Unfortunately, I quickly had to let go of that desire.

As we approached Plymouth, Mr. Thomas asked me where I would be staying that night. Before I could answer, he said they had an extra bedroom and would like me to be their guest. Pleasantly surprised by their generosity, I gladly accepted.

A short while later, we arrived at their home, a modest cottage that sat high on a cliff overlooking the ocean. A chilly, brisk wind brought in a late afternoon mist from the sea, blocking any panoramic view of the North Atlantic sunset. It seemed more like March than June to me, but I soon learned that was not unusual for England.

Sitting down to supper in their intimate kitchen, I felt welcomed. The Plymouth seaside suited me much more than the London metropolis. Relaxing for the first time since I left the States, I slipped out of my aloneness and into the lives of this simple English couple. What a relief that was.

During supper, I got to know my hosts a little. Mr. Thomas was a supervisor at the local factory that made machine tools. Mrs. Thomas took care of things on the home front. Their son, John, was studying engineering at university in London.

I explained that I'd studied law in school. Then I told them my story of becoming disenchanted with practicing law, leaving my job, and embarking on my world adventure with the hope of discovering a better life.

"That's too bad," Mrs. Thomas said sympathetically. "I hope you find what you are looking for."

"Thank you," I replied. "But I'm really not sure what I'm looking for. Hopefully, it will come to me soon."

After supper, Mrs. Thomas showed me to my room. Since we were all tired from the long drive, we soon wished each other good night and went to bed. The next morning, I awoke to the rich aroma of breakfast. Following a hearty meal of scrambled eggs, sausage, hash brown potatoes, buttered toast, and black tea, I expressed my deep gratitude to the Thomases for their kindness and generosity. Then Mr. Thomas drove me to the road heading north out of Plymouth and wished me good luck.

I took to the highway, but this time with a sense of satisfaction that I had finally connected with a genuine British couple. For once, my hungry ghost's gluttony did not interfere with my ability to be present and enjoy myself.

I traveled north through the Lake District and all the way to the magical city of Edinburgh, Scotland. In the heart of the city was its crown jewel, Edinburgh Castle. Built in 1103, this glorious, ancient icon stood tall on volcanic Castle Rock. The imposing castle looked like it came straight out of a fairytale. I imagined the King of Scotland on his white horse, followed by his entourage carrying the royal flags, riding out the front gate and over the stone drawbridge.

As much as I was impressed by Edinburgh Castle, I was even more captivated by the jovial Scottish people. I spent an evening in one of Edinburgh's local brew taverns. Singing and laughter filled the pub for hours. The more beer I drank, the better I was able to mimic the music and sing along. Raising my mug in delightful appreciation, I exchanged broad smiles with those songsters near me, as if we were lifelong friends. I had never experienced such overwhelming exuberance and camaraderie up close. That night my hungry ghost was nourished by so many lighthearted people. The joyful Scottish spirit had found a place in my heart.

From Edinburgh, I hitched a ride to Aberdeen and attended the Highland games. Nothing can compare to the International Caber Tossing Championship I witnessed there. Burly, Goliath-like men ran fifty yards cradling monstrous missiles the size of telephone poles against their bellies. With one huge "Humph," they tossed the cabers skyward—up, out, and over, if they were lucky, making a gigantic somersault in the air so the end of the caber that had been nestled in their arms now lay as far away from them as they could hurl it. The winner was the titan who threw it the farthest. If I hadn't seen it with my own eyes, I wouldn't have believed they had actually accomplished this Herculean feat.

What seemed even more incredible was that I arrived in Aberdeen with no prior knowledge that the Highland games were being held there at that exact time. I began to believe the universe worked in mysterious ways and that practically nothing happened by accident.

I didn't think a God in the heavens was pulling the strings to make everything happen according to some grand plan. Rather, I imagined a universal web of energy connected everything, creating one interdependent entity. One spark of energy automatically set off a chain reaction, which reverberated through the cosmos, causing many other events to occur. Simply put, one thing led to another, or every action caused a reaction. That domino effect resulted in my leaving my job in Trenton and ultimately landed me at the Highland games in Aberdeen. I had free will, but all my prior decisions led me to making my next choice. And that one then led me to the next.

Leaving Aberdeen the following day was no easy task. After five hours with my thumb out, two crazy Scotsmen in a mini-automobile that looked like a kid's toy finally stopped and picked me up. We had to push the damn thing backward to get it started again. Later, as it was getting dark and foggy, Roger, the driver, could barely see anything. We heard a loud, abrupt thud. A flock of sheep had been crossing the road and we had run into one of them. We got out of the car to see what had happened. Sadly, the sheep was badly injured.

"Damn sheep!" Roger shouted, as if it were the sheep's fault. "I think we have to put it out of its misery," he added, pulling out his knife to slit the poor creature's throat.

While I was freaking out, the two Scotsmen seemed to take the whole episode in stride. I guessed it wasn't the first time they had to deal with that kind of accident. I hoped I would never have to witness it again as we got back in the car and continued on our way.

A day or two later, I was on the shores of Loch Ness, the lake where the mysterious Loch Ness monster supposedly resided. Six months out of the year, manned outposts along the lake continuously watched for sightings of the elusive monster. Whether or not such a being really existed, the Scots took it very seriously, keeping detailed logs of their observations.

I spoke with one of the official Loch Ness observers. He showed me a picture of a large, dark shadow in the water that he believed was the monster lurking just beneath the surface.

Though I didn't express my doubts to him, I wasn't so sure the monster actually existed.

I loved Scotland: the hardy people, the gorgeous countryside, and its rich traditions. Yet I barely had time for a photo op. The starting date for the Eurail Pass, which I had previously purchased in Amsterdam, would soon be here. Since it would only be valid for a brief two months, I had no time to lose. Meanwhile, my hungry ghost kept egging me on as well. I was determined to get on with my search to fill my deep craving, though I knew not what that might be.

My stay in Paris was much like my visit to London, only worse since I didn't speak French. It didn't help that the French were not particularly welcoming to people who didn't speak their language. I was lonely as I visited the primary tourist sites, and after completing my tour of Paris and one last delicious crepe, I hopped on a night train to Vienna.

I was charmed by the old city with its State Opera House, St. Stephen's Cathedral, and beautiful palaces. I particularly enjoyed the bustling beer gardens filled with laughter and music that reminded me of Edinburgh. But I was in such a hurry, I didn't get to the Prater Amusement Park with its world-famous giant Ferris wheel.

What was I thinking? That my Eurail Pass would expire before I got to visit every country on the continent? My head was spinning, never stopping so I could catch my breath and take it all in. I was on a fast track through Europe and had not yet figured out how to slow down or what I was really trying to accomplish.

Finally, in the Alpine village of Grindelwald, Switzerland, I had a little respite. I loved the mountains. They spoke to me, and I knew their language. With two other Americans staying at the youth hostel, I climbed thirty-eight hundred feet to the seven-thousand-foot ridge top of Grindelwald First. The crisp mountain air and endless blue skies cleared my mind. My worries about what I would do and where I would live when I returned home quickly floated away. Surrounded by a snow-covered landscape of sharp, angular giants rising twelve to fourteen thousand feet above us, I felt a kinship with the majestic Alps as we settled down for a leisurely lunch of Swiss cheese, bread, wine, and fruit. It was a moment of heavenly bliss.

Feeling on top of the world rejuvenated me. The emptiness of long, lonely train rides and crowded cities disappeared as the still, quiet strength of the mountains penetrated my being. I was home at last in the Swiss Alps. I found a deep resting place that was truly enough, much more so than my brief but tranquil stay in Plymouth with the Thomases. My hungry ghost felt satisfied. I could have stayed in those mountains soaking up their peaceful energy for weeks, but it was not to be. The youth hostel had a three-day limit. Like it or not, I had to be on my way.

My next stop was Pamplona, Spain, for the famous running of the bulls during the Festival of San Fermin. I had to quickly switch gears and get ready for tons of excitement and loads of people. A sea of backpackers flooded the city, and anticipation filled the air. I felt like I was at the Super Bowl or a World Series game. After checking everything except my sleeping bag at the train station, I settled down among the multitudes on the banks of the Arga River. Exhausted, any place I could rest my head would do. But I could hardly sleep.

Pamplona was going to be one big party town for the next five days. Singing and dancing in the streets, small bands making music on every other corner, and drunks sprawled across the town square. All of it was preliminary to the main spectacle: the bullfights.

Five-thirty the next morning, the streets were mobbed. The avenue where the bulls would soon run was packed solid. My anticipation erupted as I spotted the bulls. People scattered to the edges of the road. The brave and the crazy ran in front of the rampaging beasts as they charged toward the arena. The madness had begun.

The bullfighting arena, the Plaza de Toros Monumental, was jammed with screaming spectators jumping up and down. Everyone was high on wine or dope or some other substance. Matadors and picadors in bright, elaborate costumes marched into the ring. One by one, six bulls were let loose to be jabbed and finally slaughtered before the raucous, blood-thirsty crowd. It was quite a show, but I didn't have the stomach for it.

Why were these poor, innocent animals being taunted and killed, I wondered. For the fun and amusement of a drunken mob? What had humankind come to? It made me sick to my stomach. One day of the ugly frenzy was more than enough for me. The next morning, I escaped on a train to Madrid.

By mid-July, I had been on the road for two months. Still, I was restless. With all my freedom and adventures, why wasn't I feeling good about my trip? Something was missing. Why wasn't I satisfied with all the fun and excitement I was having? I continued struggling as I tried to figure out the source of my discontent. What was my life about? What would give me lasting contentment?

One thing I did know: I wasn't ready to go home. Not until I got some real peace of mind. I understood that my journey was about much more than taking a summer vacation. I would not go home until I discovered what that was.

3

TRAVELING BACK IN TIME

I GOT OFF THE TRAIN in Madrid wondering where I would stay. In the train station, I met a guy named Ron Chapel from California. Since we were both on the road alone, we decided to get a room together.

Ron had just returned from the East. He had gotten as far as Pakistan when his traveling companion contracted a serious case of hepatitis and had to fly back to the States for treatment. Rather than going on by himself, he decided to head back to Europe.

That night, Ron related his tales from his time in the East. I took out my notepad and began jotting down names of towns, restaurants, and interesting sites he'd visited on his route from Turkey to Pakistan. The cave dwellings he discovered in Turkey were particularly intriguing to me. I gave them a star in my notes, hoping I would have an opportunity to explore them soon.

Ron and I shared an interest in art, so we went to Madrid's famous Prado Museum, where we were both captivated by Goya's disturbing masterpiece, *The Third of May 1808*. The painting focused on the horrors of war. It reminded us that our country was then engaged in the Vietnam War.

When we left the museum, I turned to Ron and said, "Boy, are we lucky."

"What do you mean?" he asked.

"Those poor soldiers in Goya's painting could be us in Vietnam. Somehow, we've managed to escape their fate while many other guys have not. I can't imagine being in their shoes. The whole situation drives me crazy with anger and contempt for Nixon and his cronies."

Ron nodded. "Yeah, you're right. I'd go to Canada before I'd go to Nam. We don't belong over there anyway. What a tragic mess. Sure hope McGovern wins the election and gets us out of there."

"I wouldn't count on it. We're better off here." I then told Ron how I had marched in DC and New York against the war but that I doubted it had made any difference. Still, I was glad I had. "Like practically everything we do, the primary reason we do it is to meet some need or desire we hold within us. It felt good to participate in the anti-war movement. I was standing up for what I believed was right rather than sitting quietly on the sidelines." Knowing Ron and I were on the same page about the Vietnam War made me feel more connected to him. I would have had a difficult time relating to him if he supported the war. It was an important perspective we shared.

When Ron told me he wanted to explore Morocco next, I proposed we go together. Having a traveling partner would make me feel more secure in that potentially dangerous country. A couple of days later, we were on the southern coast of Spain catching a boat to Ceuta, a Spanish port in North Africa. From there, we boarded a bus to the Moroccan border.

We were somewhat nervous about crossing the border into Morocco. Long-haired hippies were not permitted in that conservative, Muslim country. At the bus station, I went into the men's room to wet down my hair and comb it back behind my ears, tucking long strands under my collar. The only other thing I could do was cross my fingers. But one factor was in our favor. The night was extremely dark.

By the time we arrived at the border crossing, it was well past midnight. The lights were dim, and the Moroccan customs officials looked pretty tired. Before we knew it, they had given us a quick once over, stamped our passports, and approved our entry into their country. As our bus entered Morocco on our way to Tangier, we both let out a huge sigh of relief.

The next day, Ron and I adopted Abdul as our guide. He was a young kid, maybe nine or ten, who spoke enough English to help steer our way. He offered to direct us through the narrow, winding streets of the medina, the historic old city. In return, he expected a generous tip in dirham, the Moroccan currency.

We followed Abdul to a shop where we watched in awe as Moroccan artisans wove intricate patterns with multicolored threads for their rugs. I sensed that he wanted us to buy one of their beautiful rugs so he could receive a commission, but we didn't. Abdul next led us to the back of another shop, where an elderly man with a long, straggly beard quietly handed me a pipe filled with *kief*, a highly concentrated extract from cannabis that Moroccans smoked.

I took a hit. Before I knew it, I had keeled over and was flat on my back. The strong Moroccan pot packed a powerful punch. My head felt light and dizzy. After a few minutes, I regained my equilibrium, and with Ron's help, I was back on my feet, though still a bit dazed. "Whoa, that's some dope," I stammered. I had no idea how one hit of weed could be so strong.

From there, we headed to a little café for a tall glass of mint tea. The national drink, Moroccan mint tea was made by pouring steaming hot water over lush mint leaves and adding plenty of sugar. When you took a sip and closed your eyes, all your troubles floated away. It really worked for me, especially after my experience with kief.

The next morning we caught a bus to Fez, a medieval, walled city in central Morocco. Early on during the trip from Tangier to Fez, I started having sharp stomach pains and realized I was having a bad attack of dysentery. We were in the middle of nowhere in dry, barren, open territory.

"We had better get to a stop soon or I'll be shitting in my pants," I whispered to myself. Fortunately, the bus stopped, and I made it to an isolated latrine just in time to relieve myself. There were no toilets, as was true in many other places in Morocco, just a hole in the ground.

Back on the bus with more cramps, I nervously hoped we would soon get to Fez. When we finally arrived, it was not in time for me to get to another private latrine. Feeling very uncomfortable and extremely embarrassed, I smelled bad and needed to change my pants as soon as possible. But there was nothing I could do until we got to our room for the night. When we finally did, I cleaned myself up and changed my clothes.

Despite that miserable ride, I was so glad we had made it to Fez. Founded in 789, the high walls and huge gates of the ancient city protected it from invasions. Entrance into the city's intricate maze of streets was through several gigantic gates. One of the most beautiful was Bab Chorfa, "the Gate of Nobles." The stately gate was decorated with harmonious engravings and flanked by two big towers. It controlled access to the medina and was part of the Kasbah An-Nouar (which means "citadel of the flowers"), one of several fortified military enclosures or kasbahs built around the old city.

El-Bali, the larger of Fez's two medinas, was the biggest pedestrian zone in the world with its labyrinth of over nine thousand narrow streets and alleys. Roaming through them was like being magically transported more than a thousand years back in time. There were no cars or trucks, just donkeys, carts, and shoppers carrying large baskets on their heads. As they passed by me, I was amazed by their ability to balance such heavy loads while hurrying through the old city. I was in the most foreign place I had ever been in my life.

The following day was Friday, the Muslim Sabbath. The walled medina was closed while everyone went to the mosque to worship. I watched as the people entered their holy sanctuary. They carefully washed their feet before entering the mosque and washed their hands once inside the main courtyard. From the entranceway, I could sense the strong spirit of these devout people.

I was witnessing how one's faith can be a way of life. I only had a glimpse of anything like that once while I was growing up in the Jewish faith. I remembered swaying along with two hundred other Jewish teenagers in a candle-lit hall as our spirits were lifted by the mesmerizing songs of Shlomo Carlebach, the singing rabbi. But that was just a fleeting moment. I never had the ongoing deep connection to Judaism that I witnessed in these people that day. Thousands of Muslims kneeled in prayer. It was a powerful reminder of their devotion to Spirit or Allah. The holiness of the hour nourished my hungry ghost. It gave me a hint of what I might be seeking on my journey.

I began to comprehend a basic value that separated Eastern thought and life from the West. The Muslim worshippers I observed were profoundly steeped in their ageless ways. They prayed five times every day and didn't appear ready to abandon their daily rituals to gain economic opportunity or Western modernity. Their lives did not seem to be about getting ahead, moving to a nicer neighborhood, or going on vacation. Of course, like a great many Westerners, they worked to provide for their families. But I sensed that they were driven by their inner devotion rather than any outer, worldly needs or desires. I was discovering a very different way of life that made me again question my own. The hungry ghost within me was aroused. What would actually satisfy it?

A couple of days later, Ron and I headed for the train station to buy our tickets back to Tangier. Ron asked a small boy for directions. He pointed and we continued on our way, not sure if the kid had even understood our question. As we walked down the street, a Moroccan girl, probably about fifteen, ran up to us from behind.

Catching her breath, she called out in English, "My father saw you talking to my little brother. He wishes you to be his guests at our home." Thrilled and intrigued by her invitation, we readily agreed and followed her back to their humble yet neat apartment.

Her father, M. Abdallah Zi Zi, was the headmaster of a school on the outskirts of Fez. A large, robust man, he was obviously proud to have Western guests in his home, which was colorfully decorated with orange, red, and yellow Moroccan textiles. Abdallah smiled and warmly greeted us with open arms. "I am honored to have you as my guests." "Thank you. We feel honored to be invited into your home and very glad to meet you and your family," Ron replied.

Though some were shy, all the children came into the living room to greet us. Only Nadia, the girl who had stopped us in the street, spoke English. The oldest of seven children, she had studied French and English and was planning on continuing her studies in Paris.

Abdallah's wife, Farah, offered us mint soda, cookies, and watermelon. We ate and answered questions concerning our travels, occupations, and backgrounds. "What do you think of Morocco?" Abdallah asked.

"We like it very much," I replied. "We're inspired by how Moroccans maintain their ancient customs and traditions. In America, we always seem to be rushing into the future, always trying to create something new. It's so different here."

When we asked if we might take a picture of the family, Abdallah replied, "By all means." Everyone hurried to dress in their best outfits, and all the children seemed eager and delighted at the opportunity, as if they were about to appear on national TV.

A short while later, we thanked Abdallah and his family and went on our way to the train station. I thought to myself how lucky we were to be invited to Abdallah's home and meet his family. I felt fortunate to be learning up close how people lived in other parts of the world. It was one of the highlights of my journey.

The train to Tangier left at 10:00 p.m. At midnight, it arrived at Meknes, where a horde of teenage boys waited impatiently on the platform. Before the train came to a full stop, they were jumping onto the cars. In a few brief moments, the train was inundated with them. They were literally hanging from the rafters and falling into our laps. The mass of screaming boys created a frenzy that scared us. Who knew what would happen next? In the hot Moroccan night, the crush of bodies was almost unbearable. We hoped the train would pull out soon so we could at least catch a breeze. Twenty minutes later, it finally left the station.

We quickly learned the reason for the frenzy. These kids were on an outing to the ocean. They rode the night train so they would arrive in the morning and have a full day at the beach. Slowly, we began to make contact, though we had no common language. One boy passed us a pipe of kief. We offered them fruit and drinks. What first appeared to us to be a pending disaster turned out to be a moving party.

As we approached the station where we had to switch trains to Tangier, we planned our exit. Though only twenty feet away, the aisle and doors were blocked by a sea of humanity. We thought we'd never get out during the short time the train remained at the station.

Just as the train screeched to a halt, Ron jumped out the window next to our seats. It was the only way we could be sure to get off before the train started up again. The second I stood to grab our backpacks, ten screaming boys began fighting for my seat. I threw Ron's pack out the window to him. Reaching under the seat for my bulky pack, I started to panic. Would

I be able to get it and myself out the window before the train started to depart? After stuffing my pack through the window, by some small miracle, I jumped, landed on the platform, and screamed in relief as the train began moving again.

Two days later, we took the ferry back to Spain. At 2:30 a.m., after ten wild days in Morocco, we were met by Spanish customs officers. Ron and I practically had to wake them up to have our passports stamped. It would have been easy to sneak some great Moroccan hash by them, but how could we have known that? Better safe than six years in a Spanish jail.

My Moroccan adventure gave me a taste of a world totally foreign from my own. But whatever I was seeking was not in the deserts of northern Africa, though my experience at the mosque in Fez did get me thinking. My journey to that sun-baked country had a significant, residual effect: It enhanced my appetite for the unknown and strengthened my resolve to head East. My course was becoming clearer. I would travel to Italy and Greece and then on to Asia.

A few days later, Ron and I parted ways at the Barcelona train station. With a big hug, we wished each other good luck as I headed to Italy while he prepared to return home to the States. More than three weeks had elapsed since our paths first crossed in Madrid. We had been through a lot together, and I was already beginning to miss him. Having a traveling companion to share the ups and downs of the road with made my journey so much more comforting and fun. But it was time to move on. My hungry ghost demanded that I resume the quest for whatever it was I was in search of.

I arrived in Florence with mixed emotions. My college art history course compelled me to endure the August heat and throngs of tourists so I could appreciate firsthand some of the rich Italian masterpieces I had only seen slides of in class. On a hot, muggy summer day, I persevered through a tour of the Uffizi Museum with thousands of art lovers. Then I took in the Baptistery of San Giovanni where Lorenzo Ghiberti's *Gates of Paradise* was on display. Those gilded bronze doors dating back to the fifteenth century were incredible. They were seventeen feet high and consisted of ten panels. Each panel depicted an intricately detailed scene from the Old Testament, from Adam and Eve to Solomon and the Queen of Sheba. And each one was made from a single cast.

In the middle of the sweltering day, I stopped at Vivoli Ice Cream Parlour for some cantaloupe and chocolate mousse ice cream. It was the best ice cream I had ever tasted. Sometimes I wondered whether I had come to Italy for its art or its delicious ice cream and gelato. Probably all three, I concluded.

The next day I went to the Medici Chapel where Michelangelo's *Night, Day, Dawn, and Dusk* statues lived. Then the Palazzo Vecchio, the Ponte Vecchio, and the Florentine flea market all in the same day. I was beat. One of the most revered works of art in Florence would have to wait until tomorrow.

When I finally did see Michelangelo's statue of David, I knew at once that it was no ordinary masterpiece. The towering, majestic quality of the figure was overwhelming and inspiring. Yet, while I was in awe of Michelangelo's magnificent artistry, I felt my aloneness and wished I had Ron or someone else to share it with. I was learning how much I valued companionship. Afterward, I hurried back to Vivoli for some more treats to soothe my hungry ghost and bring me back down to earth.

I could not explore Italy without going to Rome, but being a tourist in Rome in the August heat was no easy assignment. My hungry ghost pushed me to see as much as possible: the

Spanish Steps, the Pantheon, the Roman Forum, the Colosseum, the Trevi Fountain, and Michelangelo's statue of Moses, which was as inspiring as his David. I was particularly taken by the Forum, the heart of Roman commerce and government when Julius Ceasar and other emperors ruled over the Roman Empire. I reflected on how far we had come since then and how far we still had to go to be a truly democratic republic. With all the corruption and greed in the US government, I was not sure how much progress had actually been made.

Later that afternoon, I could have used some assistance from a Roman emperor to get back to my pension. The traffic in Rome was outrageous. Sometimes I felt my life was in danger just trying to cross a major thoroughfare like Via Nazionale.

The following day I toured the Vatican, St. Peter's, and the Sistine Chapel. St. Peter's was by far the most lavish church I had ever seen. Every inch was elaborately decorated. Its overindulgent opulence greatly increased my disdain for the Catholic Church. I couldn't help but think about the millions of dollars it took to build and maintain this extravagant edifice while so many people had so little and struggled just to stay alive. It didn't make sense to me. So much potential for good was lost through such unimaginable excess. I shuddered in disgust.

My rush through Rome epitomized everything I had come to dislike about my tour of Europe. It was another whistle-stop attempt at happiness, overflowing with scurrying tourists like many of the other places I'd visited. While I pondered my frustration, I still had no idea what to do about it. Somehow, I would have to break this half-empty travel cycle. Escaping from its grip was becoming more important than my search for good times. But at this point, the only answer was to continue on my journey. Eventually, I would solve this puzzle, or so I hoped.

Next on my agenda was Pompeii, a whole city buried alive two thousand years ago by volcanic ash with its plumbing system still intact. The public baths, homes, and government buildings were all standing. Some had murals on their walls. Others had mosaic tiles by their front doors warning strangers to beware of the dog. A wealthy bachelor's apartment had a painting of a man holding his penis in one hand and a pot of gold in the other. The sign on the front door read "Worth its weight in gold." I reflected on the fact that the male gender hadn't changed all that much after two millennia.

I roamed through the theater, the Colosseum, and the Palestra in amazement. The casts of men and women with expressions of agony forever imprinted on their faces were arresting. It was a strange twist of nature that preserved their crying out two thousand years later. In this museum of history, I recognized that human suffering continued unabated throughout the ages, and it deeply saddened me.

As I prepared to leave Italy, I wrote to my parents telling them I was thinking of going to India and asking them to withdraw three hundred dollars from my bank account and send it to me in Istanbul. I told them I was on my way to Greece and would let them know my plans when they became clearer.

As I mailed my postcard, I wondered how they would take the news. I knew it wouldn't be good. They hadn't been crazy about my going to Europe in the first place. Now what was supposed to be a summer vacation had become something completely removed from their sphere of reference. How they would take my world traveling I couldn't predict, but I also couldn't worry much about it. I hoped they would come to understand this was my path and I just had to continue my journey.

With my final gelato in hand, I stepped onto the boat that would take me to Greece.

4

GEARING UP AND HEADING EAST

LETTING GO OF MY NEED to plan and allowing whatever arose in the present moment to guide me led to remarkable twists and turns in my life. One day I was practicing law in Trenton and then suddenly, like being transported through time and space by some supernatural machine, I was camping on a nude beach with five hippies I barely knew on the Greek island of Crete.

By the time I got to Crete, I had visited over twenty-five places in eleven countries in a little more than three months. I needed a rest, and Crete was the perfect place for that. Hanging out on this seemingly endless beach was my first opportunity to fully stop, go inward, and take stock of where I was in my life's journey. Basking in the hot sun, I read Andre Gide's *Fruits of the Earth*. His 1897 musings clearly spoke to me:

> The path that has to be chosen lies through a wholly unexplored country, when each one makes his own discoveries, and—note this—for himself alone; so that the vaguest track in the darkest Africa is more easily distinguishable… (and) we cannot see as far as the horizon…

I felt that my path, as well, lay through wholly unexplored territory that was forever changing. Still, I wondered how I had managed to land on this incredible island so far from home. Never in my wildest imagination did I think I'd be here at this point in my life.

I first met my motley travelling companions in Athens just a couple of weeks before we took off together for Crete. I was staying in the basement dormitory of the Orion Hotel with ten other low-budget wanderers, our sleeping bags spread out on the concrete floor. In the middle of a rainy, late August night, four vagabonds came barreling into our simple quarters. They practically tripped over me before someone turned on the lights.

"What the hell is going on? Knock it off," I muttered, still half asleep. Trying not to cause any further commotion, they quickly settled down and turned off the lights as the rest of us tried to fall back asleep.

The next day, Lorrie, one of the four intruders, tried to make amends for their late-night disturbance. "Does anyone want to smoke a joint?" she asked with a big smile. I nodded as she lit up a rather large doobie. In no time, we were all high and getting to know each other.

Mac, Lorrie, Toad, and Mindy, all young Americans in their twenties, had just gotten off a train from Yugoslavia the previous night. They had started from Heidelberg, Germany, the location of the US Army's European headquarters where Mac and Lorrie had been dealing drugs to the local GIs. Mac was clearly the leader of their little troop. While his voice projected authority, his straggly, dirty-blond hair and undernourished physique revealed he was not in great shape.

Short, slim Lorrie knew how to get around. She left New York after graduating from Hofstra University with a BA in English. While living in London, she and a girlfriend decided to hitchhike through Ireland. From there, she moved on to Amsterdam, where she met Mac and got involved in the drug trafficking scene.

Mac and Lorrie had spent the last six months in Heidelberg. They shuttled back and forth to Amsterdam, acquiring drugs for their business with the GIs. In the process, they got hooked on heroin and Mac came down with hepatitis. As soon as he was well enough, they gave up dealing drugs and left Germany. Their friends, Toad and Mindy, came along for the ride.

Toad was tall, lanky, and quiet. He seemed to be a nice guy, but he never had that much to say. With appealing black hair and a cute smile, Mindy was on the short side. She was kind of reserved like Toad. They were mostly into being with each other and staying out of the way. Mac and Lorrie were clearly in charge and did most of the talking.

"We're thinking about going overland to India," Mac said casually while getting high with me.

"Me too," I instantly replied. Before I knew it, we were throwing in together, buying a beat-up 1964 VW minibus with a large, orange rising sun painted on one side and planning to drive from Athens to India.

In the meantime, Ginger, a starry-eyed flower child from California who was barely eighteen, happened along and wanted to join our traveling party. I noticed her walking alone outside our hotel and was immediately taken by her big blue eyes. Ginger strolled up to me and asked where I was headed. When I told her, she gave me an inviting smile and asked if she could come too. Without considering what the others would say, I eagerly replied, "Sure." As I filled her in on our plans, I began imagining Ginger and me becoming more than friends while traveling east together.

Before we could begin the trek to India, we had to be sure our VW minibus was in good enough shape to get us there. It turned out the two hundred dollars we paid for it was not such a bargain. Our classic minibus required a major overhaul, including new tires, a valve replacement, and an additional window on one side to give those riding in the back some air and light. So we left it at a local auto repair and body shop and hopped on a boat to Crete.

My newfound friends and I arrived on Crete in early September and went straight to the breathtaking Red Beach on the south shore. It was one of the top nudist-friendly beaches on Crete, and as the name suggested, it had reddish sand. We quickly set up our seaside shelter just a few feet from the incredibly clear Aegean Sea.

Somehow, Mac, a natural trickster, had swiped a huge Yugoslavian flag while he and his troop passed through that country. It served as a splendid roof for our makeshift hut, protecting us from the intense island sun. Our collective gear included a multicolored African blanket, an oversized Spanish bedspread, and a US Army poncho. Those items formed three walls of our humble abode. An imposing gray boulder jutted out of the sand to complete the enclosure, and sturdy sugarcane stalks on each corner framed our tiny house. Unfortunately, it was only big enough for three of us to sleep in at a time. We took turns while the others slept outside on the beach.

Our colorful hut sat less than ten feet above the ocean waves crashing against the rocks below. Without running water or plumbing, the sea was our bathtub. When we wanted a hot meal, we cooked it on a one-burner camping stove.

A forty-five-minute hike over a sandy hill separated us from the fishing village of Matala, a hippie haven. A couple who could not sit still joined our beach crew and readily volunteered to make the daily trek to replenish our supplies and refill our water containers at the village store. I was happy to stay put, soaking up the sun's warm rays, reading, and taking a dip in the turquoise sea to cool off every so often. There wasn't a peep from my hungry ghost.

We shared our tropical paradise with about twenty-five antiestablishment wanderers who landed there from the four corners of the world. Australians, Germans, Japanese, Scots, French, Americans, and others created a peaceful, international community. It was quite a bohemian scene.

One moonless evening, I hung out on the hillside behind our seaside hut. The immense sky was filled with countless, sparkling stars. Relaxed, my mind began wondering as I gazed into the infinite heavens. Then I heard my hungry ghost calling out. *What am I doing here? Where do I belong?* As tranquil as everything was, I still had those puzzling questions rattling around in my head.

But this time, believing it was not yet the hour for any answers to be revealed, I was able to let go of my need to be clear about what I was doing or where I was going. Being enveloped in the serenity of the still night, my entire being rested. No need to know where I was headed. I was on my own magical mystery tour. Tears of joy dropped from my cheeks onto my chest as I marveled at the dazzling heavens above me.

Our laid-back time on Crete came to an end much too soon. After ten days on the beach, we took a ferry back to Athens to pick up our restored VW bus and make our final preparations before hitting the road to Istanbul. But we still had a lot to do. Lorrie and Mac needed to get their Iranian visas, which the rest of us had already obtained. Mac had to get an international driver's license as well.

Since Toad had worked as a civilian for the US Air Force in Stuttgart, Germany, he had an ID allowing him to use base facilities anywhere. "Hey, I can get us provisions on the Air Force base cheap," he said. "We can even get a car stereo cassette player and some tapes from the base PX."

Lorrie concurred and suggested we stock up on peanut butter and other stuff we would need while we were there.

Leaving Athens took all day. Mac and I went to the flea market to unload extra gear we didn't need or have room for with six of us in the minibus. It was dark by the time we returned to the campsite with an electric heater, old clothes, and camping equipment we were unable to sell at the market. We just left all of it at the campgrounds for someone else to use.

Though it was getting late, we were determined to leave Athens that night. So we piled into the van and headed east out of the city and onto the highway toward Turkey, gleefully singing "Ripple" along with the Grateful Dead on our new cassette player.

Two days later, we pulled into the Londra campgrounds outside Istanbul. Much to our surprise, the city did not live up to our expectations. We all thought it would be more exotic than it was. Even the name "Istanbul" had a mysterious ring to it. Where were all the snake charmers and opium dens?

For the most part, Istanbul appeared similar to most European cities. It was only the sprinkling of huge mosques with their towering minarets that gave the city its unique character. The Blue Mosque, the crown jewel of Istanbul, stood out above the rest. Built in the early sixteen hundreds, the mosque contained approximately twenty thousand hand-painted blue ceramic tiles adorning its interior walls. At night, it was a dazzling site, bathed in azure as lights framed its five main domes, six minarets, and eight secondary domes.

Still, the most exciting moment in Istanbul for me was Monday morning at the American Express office. I received seven letters from my friends and family, including one with the three hundred dollars I had asked my parents to send. While I was thrilled to receive all those letters, one brought tears to my eyes. I cried when I read how distraught my father was that I would not be coming home any time soon. I was dismayed that my travels were causing him such agony. He had very different expectations for my life and was upset that I was not coming close to meeting them. But his failure to see any redeeming value in what I was doing also saddened me.

Dad and I had a huge chasm separating us, and short of returning home, there was nothing I could do to bridge it. With my hungry ghost still craving some yet-to-be-revealed epiphany, I was not about to abandon my quest. Still, carrying the weight of my father's anguish made my search for meaning more pressing. My need to prove to him that my extended adventure was worth it became a critical aspect of my journey.

At the same time, Toad received some unfortunate news as well. His leave from his Army job had been cut short, and he was required to return to the base in Germany immediately. We were all disappointed that we would have to go on without him.

We wanted our last night in Istanbul to be memorable, so we went to a traditional Turkish bath with separate facilities for men and women. Like much of Istanbul, the baths didn't live up to our hopes. The massage was strictly a quick one, two, three job for tourists. Still, with the sauna, wash, and resting time, it turned out to be a relaxing evening. The best part was when Mac suggested a little mischief. "Hey, let's wrap these towels around us as a souvenir before we get dressed."

We quickly took the large, tasseled towels and wrapped them around our bodies beneath our clothing as we dressed. As soon as we got out the door, we ran as fast as we could, though the towels restricted our ability to really take off. When we finally stopped, Mac gave Toad and me a big thumbs up with one of his trademark devilish grins, and we had a good laugh celebrating our clever heist.

The next afternoon, we went to the Pudding Shop. Across from the Blue Mosque, it was where all the hippie freaks traveling east hung out. Many of them told us they were headed for Goa, India, for Christmas and suggested we do the same.

Then Mac and I went over to some guy's van to try his dope. An hour later, we returned to our campsite with an ounce of grass and some hash—to the delight of our merry little crew. We were surprised to find Toad lying in the back of the van and glad to see him. He had quit his job and come back to us. With everyone ready to roll, I turned on the engine and turned up the Grateful Dead on the stereo. We were heading out, singing "Truckin'" along with the band.

That night we crossed the Bosporus Strait on a ferry. At 9:00 p.m. on September 27, 1972, our zany little troop stepped off the boat and into Asia for the first time. Ecstatic, we were on the road again, heading east to India!

5

LOOKING BACK AND MOVING FORWARD

Istanbul is the only city in the world that spans two continents. When we crossed the Bosporus Strait on the ferry, we went from Europe into Asia, but we were still in Istanbul. And that letter from my parents was still weighing on my mind.

I thought about my childhood when I sometimes got the message from my mother that what I did wasn't good enough. It didn't matter if I got top grades in school or voluntarily cleaned my room without being prompted. My mother neglected to acknowledge my good deeds. But when I failed to meet her standards, she was quick to point out that what I did wasn't good enough. Ultimately, the belief that I, *myself*, wasn't good enough became embedded in my psyche.

I'd pretty much always had the feeling that things could be better. Whether it was my life, the nation, or the world, wherever I looked, I thought things should be better. And I believed that it was my responsibility to help make them so. That resulted in my focusing more on what I perceived was wrong or insufficient, rather than what was right or satisfactory. So I formed a pretty negative perspective on life.

Ironically, that sense of not being enough was a significant factor that propelled me forward and landed me in India. I quit my legal services job because I felt it wasn't good enough and I wasn't making enough of a difference in my clients' lives. I left Trenton because there wasn't enough for me there. And I took off on my world travels because I was dissatisfied with my life in America. Then, in Europe, my hungry ghost kept reminding me that I wasn't getting enough out of my trip.

Before I arrived in Greece in August 1972, I was already thinking my trip wasn't fulfilling. I began searching for what would make it better. During that summer, I'd met a guy whose tales about his trek to the summit of Mt. Kilimanjaro in Tanzania fascinated me. I pictured myself at the peak gazing at the sun rising on the eastern horizon. At 19,431 feet, Kilimanjaro was the highest mountain in Africa and the highest, single free-standing mountain above sea level in the world. *Wouldn't that be something?* I thought, imagining myself on top of the world. But considering my mindset and my hungry ghost lurking over my shoulder, I doubted whether that would have made my journey good enough.

So I went east from Greece, in part because my summer experience hadn't been satisfying enough. I knew there was more for me to discover on my journey, and I could not go home without finding out what that was. Plus, I couldn't get

India out of my mind. The evening I'd spent with my former girlfriend and her husband before taking off for Europe had left a strong impression that India held secrets I needed to explore. That feeling was reinforced by the Beatles' music and their well-publicized spiritual journey to India. Even more alluring was learning about Harvard professor Richard Alpert, who had immersed himself in Eastern spirituality and become the New Age guru, Ram Dass.

By the end of the summer, I knew India would be my destination. While I had briefly mentioned this in an earlier letter to my parents when I asked them to send me more money, I agonized over how to explain my decision in a way that wouldn't devastate them, especially my father. He was heavily invested emotionally in my becoming a successful attorney. The son of a modest tailor, Dad knew the hardships of the working class. As a successful dentist, he wanted me to have the security and social standing a professional career provided. But in his eyes, I was lost and moving further and further away from his hopes for my future.

One evening at a campsite in Turkey, I sat down and wrote my folks this letter:

Dear Mom and Dad,

 I got one letter from you in Istanbul, but it really didn't say much. I expected some reaction to my going East, but there was hardly any. I imagine that you weren't very happy about it. I really wish I could get you to understand.

 I've been doing a lot of thinking that I should have done years ago. The fact that it's come now makes it that much more difficult. But I feel that it is a necessary part of my growth and development. And I definitely feel that I'm learning and growing.

I don't know what the outcome of this trip will be, but I believe that it is helping me to better define myself. Helping me to get to know myself. By the time it's over, I think I'll have a much stronger grasp of who and what I am. The last few years have brought a great deal of uncertainty in that respect. Now I feel things are beginning to come together again.

I still don't know what I want to do when I get back, but whatever it is, I think it will be with a lot of energy and enthusiasm. It may be law, or it could be some type of business. A couple people I'm traveling with would like to start an import business. Right now it's a dream, but not an impossible one. Anyway, we'll have to wait and see what happens. But I am optimistic about the future.

One thing that concerns me in the present is you. I think about you and how you feel about me and what I'm doing. I know there's mixed feelings of concern, disappointment, worry, and frustration. I really don't know what to do about it except write letters like this and try to communicate with you. One thing I can't do is change or be what you want me to be just because you would like me to be a certain way. I hope you understand that at least. I must work out my life in my own way, just as every conscious, thinking individual must. If that causes you disappointment or pain, I am truly sorry. But that is the way it must be. Never, however, have I, or will I, do something in order to hurt you. I do love you and worry about you probably about as much as you worry about me.

Well, again, I am making an attempt to reach you. I feel our relations were pretty strained before I left. (I remember writing that once before.) It bothered me a lot and still does. I would really like to feel close to you and understood by you. But I don't see you trying. Especially you, Dad. I just get your disappointment and frustration. I don't know what else to say. I know there's hurt pride involved. But I'm still your son and you are my father and mother. I am not about to reject you.

Love,
Bruce

Though I poured my heart out to my parents, I received very little in the way of a meaningful response from them. There was nothing I could do about that. I just had to continue on my journey and hope our relationship would eventually improve.

I later learned that my letters to my folks actually made things worse. Each letter they received only made my dad, in particular, more distraught because it reminded him of how far his son had gone astray from his desires and dreams for me.

My parents and I had not been very close, but my extended trip separated us even more. We never had what I would call heart-to-heart talks. We did some things together while my sister and I were growing up, like family trips to Florida and Williamsburg, Virginia. Though I wasn't very good at it, I played some golf with my dad. And occasionally, we'd watch TV together in the evening—shows like *Ed Sullivan* and *Father Knows Best*. But I didn't confide in my parents, and they didn't ask me anything personal about my life. Except, of course, when I started to go out with girls, Dad warned me to use contraceptives.

When I went off to college and law school and then got my first lawyering job, I was in step with my parents' expectations. But when I quit Legal Aid in Trenton, they got a hint that some unrest was brewing in my life. My trip overseas might have been seen as just a little time out, but my letter was a clear indication that it was much more than that.

Meanwhile, I was having the time of my life, getting high and being free of work concerns or worrying about the future. I even had a little romance to spice things up. One night in the middle of Turkey, Ginger and I became more than road buddies. Along with Toad, it was our turn to sleep in the VW bus. To my surprise, Ginger cuddled up very close to me. In no time, we were making soft, loving, mushy sounds together. After a few minutes, Toad couldn't take it anymore and split. Ginger and I had a good laugh and then went back to making sweet love.

But true to her flower child nature, Ginger just wanted to have fun. She could be angelic one day and bitchy the next. I never knew what was coming next with her, and I couldn't figure out whether she was playing me or if that was just who she was.

One night we drove until it was pretty late. We were in central Turkey in an area called Cappadocia. Mac pulled off the highway and into what seemed like an enchanted desert. We were surrounded by cone-shaped rock formations that resembled giant creatures from another planet. In the black of night, these strange configurations generated an unnerving atmosphere. When we settled into one of the numerous cave dwellings nearby, the eerie vibe made it difficult for me to fall asleep.

We woke up the next morning to find a group of curious Turkish schoolboys surrounding our minibus. They sat on nearby rocks and watched as we washed up and got ready for breakfast. Becoming surer of themselves, a few boys offered us tomatoes and melons they had picked from a nearby field. We thanked the boys and invited them to have breakfast with us. As I learned again and again on our journey, sharing food was a universal sure bet for breaking the ice with strangers.

After breakfast, the Turkish boys went off to school, and we explored this strange fantasy land called the Açık Saray, which means "open palace." The area covered less than 0.4 square miles and included eight cave complexes. It dated back to somewhere around the twelfth century. Carvings and parts of frescos still remained on the cave walls. One room had pillars and others had shelves and windows. I later discovered that they were probably home to craftsmen and traders. In daylight, the landscape reminded me of the Badlands near the Black Hills in South Dakota. Rocky spires and mounds rose up to be parched by the blazing sun, and then fell into narrow crevices, forming a natural rhythmic pattern. Pinks, greens, and grays all blended together.

Dinner that night was a real treat as well. We stopped in Nevşehir and were coaxed into a restaurant on the main square. Four people waited on us as though we were in one of the finest New York restaurants. Three bottles of wine, nuts, liqueurs, and fruit, all on the house. It was a meal fit for a king for which I paid dearly later that night, puking and shitting intermittently for hours. I figured that's what happens when you have too much of a good thing.

Still, I felt it was worth it. Even more so because I was learning an important lesson: People's generosity is not based on their wealth. Rather, their generosity is a measure of their compassion and love for humanity. As I traveled through poor, third-world countries, time and time again I saw people with so little willing to share whatever they had. While it boggled my mind, my spirit soared.

The next evening, more frolicking in Zelve, another cave city with just one restaurant for tourists. Being it was off-season, we were the only ones there. As was her custom, Lorrie started getting friendly with the locals back at the bar. After a bottle of wine and some vodka, we were invited to a bachelor party in nearby Avcilar. We enjoyed a night of wine, hash, food, music, and dancing in a tiny stone hut with thirty or forty merry Turks and a few more traveling hippies. An old man played the clarinet while his backup beat the bongos. Those Turks sure knew how to have a good time.

Our little clan, on the other hand, was having serious difficulty staying on a high note. While we had fun together, the hassles with each other had become practically routine. When to eat? Where to go? What to do?

"She never does anything to help."

"We've got to have a plan. That's why nothing ever gets done around here."

"Nobody ever makes a decision."

"Toad and Mindy are in a hurry to get to Afghanistan and India. I want to relax and take it slow."

"I'm tired of being surrounded by fifty Turkish kids everywhere we go. I want some peace and quiet."

"It all seems so petty."

"They never listen to me anyway."

And on and on. We badgered each other until Mac threw in a stern reprimand. "Fuck all you people. I haven't had a decent rap with any of you since we left. It was disgusting today at the campsite. Everyone shut off in little cliques. No one ever talks to anybody around here."

Ginger had been thinking of splitting for some time. I really couldn't blame her, though she'd been as much a part of the problem as the rest of us. We tried talking it over. One night we even dragged Toad and Mindy out of bed to get us all together to work it out, but nothing came of it. Another time we all sat in the van with the rain pounding on the roof, attempting to resolve our group conflicts and making only slight progress. Mac would still be sarcastic, and Ginger would have her moods. Sooner or later, something had to give.

After a few more days on the road, we reached Malatya in eastern Turkey. Ginger and I sat down on a wall and again were immediately surrounded by a sea of young, curious, friendly Turkish boys. There must have been fifty of them crowded around us. Everywhere we went, we were the center of attention, the biggest show in town after town.

Camping on the outskirts of Tunceli, we were treated to more Turkish hospitality. A couple of men caught fish for us, gathered wood, built a fire, and cooked the fish. Then we all sat around the fire and had dinner together. The folks in the heartland of Turkey were some of the most welcoming people I'd ever encountered.

While driving through the mountains of eastern Turkey, we met a few hippies who turned us on to some Afghani hash. The stash we had picked up in Istanbul only lasted a few days, so we were excited to get high after almost two weeks with nothing to smoke except cigarettes. Getting stoned put everyone in a better frame of mind and brought our gang a little closer together, at least for a little while.

On the evening of October 6, we reached the border town of Doğubayazit. Along the way, we passed a van coming back from the East that had broken down. The fellow driving the van had been there since the previous morning along with a Turkish cop who was protecting him from Kurdish bandits. The Kurds didn't recognize the sovereignty of the Turkish government. They were an ornery tribe you wouldn't want to run into on a lonely country road. That was one of the rare times I felt scared as I traveled through very unfamiliar territory.

We awoke the next morning to the sounds of more Turkish school kids once again examining our minibus. More alarming was the convoy of Turkish tanks passing by. We were only a few kilometers from the Russian and Iranian borders. Rising from the Turkish plains to seventeen thousand feet, the snow-capped Mt. Ararat separated us from Russia. Ararat was the mountain in the Bible where Noah supposedly landed his ark after a forty-day global deluge. The imposing peak provided the Turks with some protection from their intimidating neighbors.

After fifteen days of driving through Turkey, we were ready for new horizons. While rain and hail pelted down on our van, we could see the sun shining on the distant plains. From the gloomy, gray storm, what lay ahead appeared to be a dreamland covered by a golden haze. Behind us sat Turkey. Ahead of us, Iran. High on good Afghan hash, we drove toward the sun and the mysteries of ancient Persia.

6

RIDING THE
TWISTS AND TURNS

Everything didn't come up roses for us in Iran. We'd barely crossed the border and made it through customs when our minibus started grumbling and losing power. After a couple of hours of Toad's fooling around under the hood, we hailed down a truck. Luckily, the driver agreed to tow us to Marand, which was 140 kilometers down the road, for only a thousand rials, or about fourteen dollars.

We spent the night in a Marand hotel for less than a dollar each. While it wouldn't have met Hilton's standards, it was adequate for a one-night stay. We were even fortunate enough to be able to take showers there. The next morning, we learned that we would have to take our minibus to Tabriz to get it fixed. While Toad and Mac made the towing arrangements, Ginger and I went to the bank together. It felt like I was walking with the Great Blond Queen of the West. Everyone stopped and stared. I knew it wasn't me they were gazing at.

A few men actually reached out and tried to grab Ginger. "Fucking bastards," she yelled as a hand disappeared into the crowd. Ginger hadn't realized that being a young Western woman in Islamic Iran would be so challenging. Arab men considered Western women easy because their clothes often exposed their arms and legs, unlike Muslim women who were required to be covered from head to toe in some Arab countries. But Ginger was not about to conform to Muslim law or customs. She was as strong-willed as they come.

Since we were stuck in Tabriz while the van was being repaired, we tried to make the best of it. One afternoon, Ginger and I went wandering in the bazaar. When a bright, multicolored cloth caught her eye in one of the open-air stalls, she visualized herself dressed in it. One hundred rials was the asking price.

"Forty," I said to the merchant, writing it down so as not to be misunderstood.

"Eighty," he countered.

"Forty-five," I fired back.

"Seventy."

"Sixty," I said, thinking it was my final offer.

"Sold!" he replied.

It wasn't exactly like shopping at Macy's, but it was a hell of a lot more fun. Best of all, Ginger was ecstatic and gave me one of her irresistible smiles.

A few days later, the van was finally ready, and we were back on the road again. The next afternoon, we arrived at a campground outside Tehran. That evening called for a celebration.

Using Toad's military pass to enter the US Army installation, we went to the base cafeteria and we each ordered a big steak dinner with all the trimmings. Having endured the VW bus breakdown and being stuck in Tabriz for several days, we felt we absolutely deserved to indulge ourselves.

The next day we got another delightful treat. Alongside the curb, Lorrie spotted some familiar-looking plants bending in the wind. Marijuana was growing there on the street like it was just any ordinary weed. Lorrie jumped out of the van and immediately began harvesting the crop. A local cop passing by didn't seem to care at all. Distracted by our unexpected discovery, we barely noticed him either.

Back at our campsite, we dried and crushed the grass. Five minutes later, we were getting stoned. It wasn't the greatest pot, but no one seemed to care. Having had just a little hash in eastern Turkey since leaving Istanbul, anything was better than nothing.

Our luck was also getting better in other ways. We met some friendly university students in Tehran. Behrouz and his brothers lived in a five-room, air-conditioned, fully furnished apartment with a private patio for just a hundred dollars a month. They even had a live-in manservant who cooked and cleaned for them. The students spoke English and were glad to hang out and show us around.

A modern city, Tehran had all the amenities of most big American towns. An added treat was going to see a Hollywood movie, *The French Connection*. But after a few relaxing days with our new Iranian friends, it was time to get back on the road to India once again.

A day out of Tehran, Ginger started complaining about terrible headaches that had been bothering her for the last several days. She explained that she has chronic mastoiditis, a bacterial infection that caused swelling and redness around her ear and gave her bad headaches. Almost in tears from the pain, Ginger decided she had to go back to Tehran to have the fluid that was causing her extreme discomfort drained from behind her ear.

I couldn't let her go by herself. She was a young, attractive woman, and we'd already seen demonstrations of how Arab men perceived her. So Ginger and I took the six-hour bus ride back to Tehran to get her medical care. The others continued east to Mashhad, where we would catch up with them once Ginger felt better.

In Tehran, Ginger and I stayed with Behrouz and his brothers. Once again, they made us feel right at home. Ginger went to the hospital and had her ailment checked out. The doctor told her she didn't have a fluid buildup. Rather, she had an infection of the duct leading from her nose to her ear. The doctor prescribed antibiotics and nose drops, which he assured her would eliminate the infection.

That night, I did some contemplating and recorded these reflections in my journal:

> Plodding along on the way to Afghanistan. Good times, bad times. Hassles with the people I'm traveling with. Toad and I clash every once in a while. We don't seem to have much in common except a stubborn streak. Lorrie and I also have our occasional differences, but I think we genuinely like each other and usually work it out. I keep telling her she talks too much, and the other night it got to her. I meant it as constructive criticism, but she didn't seem to take it that way.

Once in a while, Mindy and I recognize each other. More often we're strangers traveling together. I respect her solitude and admire her remarkable calm and quiet. But there are times when I feel she should be with the group. Not special times. She just doesn't seem to be with us most of the time. Her world and ours don't come together often enough. She's in another place somewhere.

When Mac and I look each other in the eye, all the bullshit falls away. Everything is on the line, clear, and to the point. Unfortunately, we don't communicate like that often enough, but it's good when we do. If Mac is in a bad mood, I find him unapproachable and stay away. I would like to be able to reach him and help him work it out. But he'd rather let it build inside. I hope I never see him burst. He can be so good—generous, honest, warm, and sincere. Yet the potential for violence lingers in the background. If he could only get rid of that malignancy.

Ginger—still an enigma. We talk and laugh and joke. She'll tell me her life's history. I think I know most of it already. And she comes to me for comfort and, occasionally, love. She knows I can't resist her. I can only reach her when she wants to let me. And I can rarely tell when that is. Most of the time, I am afraid of what her reactions to me might be. A very unstable relationship to say the least. Baffling and very frustrating. I'd let go if I could, but that certain smile keeps drawing me back. Bewitched!

The next day, after thanking Behrouz for his generous hospitality, Ginger and I caught a bus heading east. The twenty-hour ride to Mashhad gave me more time to mull over what I was doing and why: Where was I going? Afghanistan, India, Nepal. So what? Different people, different places, new experiences. Everything kept changing. Yet everything seemed to stay much the same. Again, I turned to my journal because my hungry ghost would not leave me alone.

> What am I doing? When will I stop? Going from one merry-go-round to another. Trapped in Trenton. Trapped in Boston. Trapped in Europe. Trapped in the East? Will I ever escape? Where to? Spinning, spinning, spinning.
>
> How to find contentment. It's all in the mind. Not in Trenton. Not in India. How do I grasp it and hold onto it? Sometimes I can feel it, almost see it. Reach out and it quickly slips away. Relax. Take it easy. Let it come to you. No sense running around in search of contentment. But I need something to hold onto. Someone to lighten the burden. Two can make it much easier than one. No sense trying to do it all yourself. But you've got to when there is no one there to help.
>
> Keep trying to reach out and touch people. They need me as much as I need them. Why are so many so blind? Walls, prejudices, pride, vanity, ego. Where are love, warmth, generosity, tenderness, and understanding?
>
> Truck on. Slowly, slowly change will come. Get yourself together and things will start coming together around you. Just stay calm and keep working at it.

The path is there. Follow it and all will be well someday. Someday!

Ginger and I arrived in Mashhad and immediately hailed a taxi to the Afghan consulate to get our visas. Afterward, our newfound Iranian friend, Ali, helped us find a room for the night. Ali had approached us as soon as we got off the bus. As I traveled through Eastern countries, I quickly learned that young locals were eager to give a helping hand to Westerners in anticipation of being nicely rewarded for their efforts.

Two fellow Americans, Tom and Kevin, whom we had met on the long bus ride from Tehran, agreed to share the room with us. No sooner were we settled in our room than we discovered that Ali had been showing Mac and the gang around Mashhad for the last couple of days. He told us where they were staying.

It just so happened that Ali's father sold Persian rugs. Ali helped his father by making friends with Westerners and bringing them to his dad's shop as prospective customers. After visiting with Ali's dad, Mac, Lorrie, and Toad were exploring the possibility of establishing a wholesale business importing Persian rugs to the States. They were wild about the idea.

After dinner, Kevin, Tom, Ginger, and I headed back to our room. The two guys told us they wanted to get to India as quickly as possible. Unbeknownst to me, on the bus from Tehran, Ginger had decided to go with them. The way she had suddenly gotten tight with them made me suspect something like that might be in the works. Rather than trying to change Ginger's mind—a near impossibility—I decided to see if I could join them as well.

If I were ever going to realize my dream of trekking in the Himalayas, it would have to be before the winter cold set in.

Since they were trying to get to Delhi as quickly as possible, hooking up with them might save me some time. I really didn't know how long Mac and his crew were thinking it would take them to get to India. Kevin and Tom seemed like a better bet for getting there faster.

"Hey, mind if I joined you?" I asked.

"Sure, why not?" Kevin replied.

Life on the road could change pretty damn fast, especially traveling with Ginger.

Later that evening, Mac, Lorrie, Toad, and Mindy came by our hotel room. When they walked in, I had the feeling that they had some heavy news. I began to stutter as I attempted to tell them our new plans.

Ginger interrupted. "What he's trying to say is that we've decided to go to India with Tom and Kevin."

Mac sighed in relief. "Well, that sure takes a load off our shoulders. We came to tell you that we didn't think you should be on the bus anymore. Everything has been a lot less confusing the last few days while you were in Tehran. It's much easier with just four in the van."

Ginger and I were stunned. Mac sounded like they were blaming us for all the hassles we'd had from Athens to Tehran. Ginger's feelings were hurt and she began to cry. Mac tried to mellow our parting by getting everyone stoned. But when they left later that night, there were no farewell kisses, no good luck handshakes or hugs. Just a slight hesitation and a last smiling glance from Mac as he turned to close the door behind him.

I had my regrets but no hard feelings. We knew things weren't working with all of us squeezed together in that small minibus. Some tried more than others, but still the hassles kept popping up. At times, it seemed we were making progress. It just wasn't enough.

In the middle of an August night in Athens, Mac and his gang stumbled into the basement of the Orion Hotel where I was staying. Two months later, they quietly slipped out of our dingy Mashhad hotel room. Just like that, they were gone. We might see them again somewhere down the road, I thought, as they disappeared into the mysterious Iranian darkness.

7

DISCOVERING A TRULY FOREIGN COUNTRY

I'D BEEN STONED EVER SINCE I got off the bus in Herat three days earlier. Afghan hash was the best. Being stoned from waking up in the morning till hitting the sack at night was a new experience for me. Back in the States, I got high occasionally. Now it was my constant state of mind. Not only did I feel lighter and more easygoing, but my hungry ghost quickly vanished as soon as I lit up. There was no need to search for some deeper meaning to my journey. I was having a good time in the present moment, and that was all that mattered.

There was just one thing on my mind: Ginger. We were barely still together. She had a well-developed habit with guys. She loved to play around. I barely got to know Tom and Kevin before they fell out of favor with her and were gone. She never did tell me what happened. I chose to stick with Ginger rather than go to Kabul with them. Though we had drifted apart and not slept together in weeks, I had a difficult time letting go. She had me on a string that was slowly unravelling.

We quickly had new traveling partners: Mike and Steve, two English fellows. Ginger had an innate, feminine talent for attracting the attention of men. She'd met them on the bus from Mashhad to the Iranian border town of Taybad. The four of us were in a dingy hotel on a dirt street across from the Herat bus station. There was a hitching post out front where you could tie your horse, just like in an old Western movie. Except for the commercial trucks and buses going by on their way to the next town and the dark-skinned men wearing turbans, it was much like being in one of those flicks. Donkeys and horses kicked up dust while the men wearing turbans meandered across the street carrying their rifles. I was so stoned that everything, including myself, appeared to be moving in slow motion.

Our room consisted of four woven fiber cots on wooden frames with no mattresses, a small wooden table, and a couple of chairs. All for just twenty afghanis per person a night. That was twenty-seven cents apiece. But that wasn't all we got for a little more than a quarter. As soon as we settled into our room, Rafi, the hotel manager, invited us into his private quarters to smoke hash with him. He told us the hash was number one from Mazar-i-Sharif, the hash capital of the world.

Rafi greeted us in broken English while shaking my hand. "Hello, my friend. How are you, my friend. Sit down, my friend."

He was so courteous and friendly that I thought he must be a con man. Then he sold us a five-inch by seven-inch block of hash for a mere five dollars. A chunk that size back home would have cost hundreds of dollars, if not more. I was blown away. After that he exchanged our money. Rafi was so kind and well-meaning, I couldn't help but like the happy-go-lucky, short, stocky fellow. He even allowed us and others staying in the hotel to use his personal water pipe.

Out on the street, I felt I was in a very foreign country far removed from anything I'd ever experienced before, even more so than Fez in Morocco. I passed merchants sitting lazily by their goods, which flowed out onto the dirt walkway lining the streets. They waited for customers or just someone to talk to. Fruits and vegetables in open baskets, often covered with flies, were weighed on scales balanced by pieces of spare metal. I could barely stand the somewhat rancid smell of it and wondered how the people could survive eating such tainted produce.

A boy in tattered clothing yelled, "Baksheesh. Baksheesh," with his hand out hoping to collect coins from anyone passing by. I was afraid I would be surrounded by kids asking for more if I gave him some. But I couldn't resist this cute little fellow with his big brown eyes and outstretched hand, so I reached into my pocket to find a few afghanis to drop into his palm. His smile made my day as I hurried along to avoid being mobbed by more irresistible beggars.

Back at the hotel, Steve was making lunch while Mike rolled a joint of hash mixed with tobacco. We'd been getting stoned all day because the hash was so cheap. Drugs were everywhere. One day Mike, Ginger, and I were taken to a small opium den by a guy who worked at the hotel. Two men were lying on their sides, each holding a long pipe with a bulbous shape at one end. They placed a pinch of black tarry opium in the bowl at the end of the pipe stem and lit it. As they drew on their pipes, the vapor from the melted opium traveled up the stem and into their mouths.

We readily agreed to take a couple of tokes. As soon as I did, I began to feel sick. I ran toward the john, puking before I could get there. I later learned that many opium smokers threw up after their initial toke. After that, I felt pleasantly light-headed and a bit like I was floating. In fact, most of the time I'd been in Afghanistan, I'd had the sense of gliding through time and space like a beam of light. Hash and opium could do that to you. It was an intense high that kept me wanting more.

A couple of days later, we finally got it together to head to Mazar-i-Sharif. We woke early to catch the 7:00 a.m. public transport to Maymana, a two-day journey that would bring us two-thirds of the way to our destination. At only two hundred afghanis or roughly $2.60 each, we thought the fare was quite a bargain. We got on board the open bed of what appeared to be an old Russian Army personnel carrier. A bench lined three sides of the truck bed where fourteen passengers could sit comfortably. Steve, Mike, Ginger, and I were squeezed in with a German couple and about fifteen Afghan men carrying their rifles and tons of baggage.

Dusty, bumpy, hot, cold, and windy, it was the most incredible journey I had ever taken. Up narrow mountain roads, then no roads, just open, high desert plains. An old man sitting on the truck bench across from me stared at me. Not having any common language, I stared back at him. When I saw his wrinkled face begin to form a big grin, I broke into a smile. My anxiety at being surrounded by armed Afghan men began to subside, and I felt safer. When some of them began chanting and praying, I relaxed and got into what a rough and wild ride this was.

That afternoon we drove into a huge canyon radiant with red, purple, brown, and green rock formations. Towering, deep-purple cliffs hung over my left shoulder. Trucks in front of us kicked dust in our faces while the warmth from the bright sun took the chill out of the air. My butt was raw from the bumpy ride on the hard wooden bench and my back ached. Crunched together, there was nowhere to stretch my legs. Someone was sitting on my feet. When we hit a bump, I flew a foot up off the bench. Bruised and very tired the later it got, I wondered when we would stop. I desperately needed relief.

The four of us eventually huddled together under Ginger's sleeping bag in the back of the truck. We were cold, hungry, and numb with pain as the starry night dragged on. Finally, at two in the morning, we stopped at a chai house outside of Bala Murghab, a modern town built near the ruins of the medieval city of Marw al-Rudh in northwestern Afghanistan. After some hot chai and rice with raisins, we crawled into our sleeping bags on the carpets of the chai shop and fell asleep.

But not for long. At seven that morning, we threw our packs back on the truck and prepared to leave. I turned to Ginger. "Have some chai to keep warm."

"No, I think it's rude," she replied.

It was Ramadan, the holy month when Muslims fasted from sunrise to sunset. Ginger wouldn't eat or drink in front of our fellow Muslim Afghan travelers.

I tried again. "But it's good and will warm you up."

She stubbornly rejected my offer, but a couple of hours later, she was eating fruit in the back of the truck in front of all the Afghan men. Somehow, it was no longer rude.

After a hot, rocky, dusty morning drive, we stopped at a village chai shop in the middle of nowhere. Our truck was the only vehicle there. It must have been market day. Afghan men in flowing white robes and turbans with their rifles over one shoulder, riding white horses, crowded the dirt road. I felt whisked back in time hundreds of years. The men stared at me like I was from another planet. I tried not to stare back. A few weathered old men sitting by their wares looked like prehistoric cave dwellers.

Unlike its neighboring countries, Afghanistan had never been overseen by Western powers. On its western border, Iran had been a close ally of the United States ever since the CIA organized a coup overthrowing the democratically elected government of Mohammad Mosaddegh in 1953. Pakistan and India to the east of Afghanistan were under British rule for many years until they gained independence in 1947. But no Western country ever controlled Afghanistan. Without such influences, it remained a tribal land living by its own customs and traditions dating back thousands of years. In many ways, it was a country that had never entered into the modern era.

Fortunately for us, the Afghans did use some modern devices. A couple of hours on the road after lunch, our truck broke down. We were stuck many miles from any help. Within an hour, a small jeep came, and my three traveling companions and I gratefully jumped into the jeep. The truck driver apparently had called for assistance on a walkie-talkie. I guessed he wanted to be sure his Western passengers got to Maymana safely. But we were not there yet.

I sat in the front next to the driver. Ginger, Mike, and Steve were in the back. It was getting near dusk and more difficult to see the surrounding landscape when the driver leaned over and opened the glove compartment. I was shocked when he pulled out a pistol and handed it to me. While I had learned to shoot a rifle in the Army Reserves during basic training at

Fort Dix several years earlier, I had never held a revolver in my hands before.

Suddenly, our lives were in danger. I turned to see my travelling companions in the back seat, clinging to each other in fear. I could hardly believe what was happening. I quickly pulled myself together and overcame the panic running through my body. I realized what I was being called to do. Since the driver and I had no common language, I could get no guidance from him. But I had heard about bandits assailing people traveling across Afghanistan, some of whom were even killed. Now that could be our fate as well.

I was riding shotgun. I nervously gripped the revolver as I silently prayed I would not have to use it. Still, we were in Afghanistan's version of the Wild West. At any moment, armed bandits could appear on the top of a nearby ridge ready to attack us. This was not my imagining an old Western movie again. I was living it in terrifying real time. The next two hours were the longest, most harrowing I had ever experienced in my life.

8

HANGING OUT IN KABUL

FORTUNATELY, WE MADE IT SAFELY to Maymana that evening without incident. The next day, we went on to Mazar-i-Sharif. After a few stoned days enjoying the best hash I had ever smoked, we continued on to Kabul. We got a room at the Delaram Hotel, one of several hippie hangouts in the city. Dinner at Sigi's Restaurant next door was the best veggie meal we'd had in a long time. The tea was free, and they even played rock 'n' roll. The restaurant had no furniture, just Afghan rugs covering the floor, plus plenty of shaggy wanderers from all over the world. Sigi's was the in place for free spirits in Kabul. We felt right at home and loved it.

I got a letter from my dad while I was in Kabul. He wanted to know when I was coming back to the States, if ever. "To say that I don't understand how you're living and why you're staying so long is putting it mildly," he wrote. "All we can do is hope and pray that you're OK. Don't get sick and come back soon." He signed it, "Love, Dad." I wondered if he really meant that.

I felt sad reading my dad's letter but not homesick. I had been away for almost six months. Going back home kind of frightened me. What would I do back there? I didn't even want to think about it. But Dad's letter made me consider how I might put a new life together when I returned, maybe in the spring. Could I get into something I really enjoyed doing? Could I make my dream come true, though I still had no idea what that dream might be? After many weeks content to just live in the moment, I could suddenly feel my hungry ghost rising up in me.

I was reminded of what Andre' Gide wrote in *Fruits of the Earth*, which I had read on the beach in Crete back in September. He wrote of uncertainty when we are on our path and the terror of having to choose. I deeply related to his dilemma. The more I opened myself up to all the possible choices, the more I was tormented by the uncertainty of my path. Until then, I had been masking my fear with drugs and fun times, distracting myself from exploring the depths of my agony and doubt. But for me to take the journey and succeed, I had to free myself of what had kept me tied up and contained—my swaddling clothes, as Gide put it—or I would be unable to move forward. Gide likened the path of growth to the winged seeds of a sycamore that travelled some distance from the tree. They needed their own rich soil, freed from the shade of the tree from whence they had come.

I asked myself why my father couldn't see that this was how my life had to be. I had to bolster my self-confidence and find my way alone. All I required was a little faith in where my path would lead me. Otherwise, I would be doomed to life on a treadmill, going nowhere. Could my future be better than that? I needed the courage to take the path of growth and find out.

I arrived in Kabul on October 31, Halloween back in the States. Occasionally during my travels, I thought about where I was last year at that particular time. The previous Halloween, I was substitute teaching in an Arlington, Massachusetts, junior high school. Now, a year later, my life had been turned upside down in *almost* every way imaginable.

Hanging out in Sigi's restaurant, I listened to the Beatles singing "I am the Walrus." I loved hearing the Beatles. Halfway around the world, their musical magic hadn't changed. We were all together hanging out at Sigi's, having a great time with no worries, no responsibilities. Just being in the moment, detached from the world outside our own little hippie heaven. And my hungry ghost was nowhere in sight.

Meanwhile, not much had changed in America. The day after the presidential election, I went to the US embassy to learn that President Nixon had been reelected. Utterly disheartened by George McGovern's crushing defeat, I was glad not to be back there.

Then, a couple of days later, I was struck by another tragic event in the hotel where we were staying. An American woman died after spending most of the night in the hotel's opium den. It freaked me out because I'd seen her there that same evening stoned out of her mind.

The place was dark and smokey with large, purple cushions covering the floor. I took off my shoes at the door like everyone else. Several customers were reclining on soft pillows and holding thin, foot-long opium pipes. They all appeared to be in drug-induced stupors from inhaling opium vapor. The woman, probably in her thirties, looked really spaced out to me before she even began smoking. She'd likely been doing some other drugs as well. When I left the den at midnight, she'd been smoking opium for well over an hour. I heard she was still at it when the den closed at three in the morning.

All the opium dens in Kabul were shut down after that. The next day, an Afghan kid who worked in the hotel came to our room and informed us that the police had arrested someone on drug charges. He warned us that we shouldn't smoke hash anymore. That was unlikely. While we were cautious and only smoked in our room from then on, we weren't about to give up getting high altogether. It had become as much a part of our daily routine as drinking water or getting something to eat.

Kabul was a hippie paradise. The Afghans and the stoners had a symbiotic relationship. We created lots of business for the hotels and restaurants. They provided a cheap, comfortable lifestyle for us in return: exotic food, decent places to crash, good music, and plenty of hash, all for a dollar or two a day. I was living an enchanted life for almost nothing. Since arriving in Afghanistan, my hungry ghost had once again disappeared.

Unfortunately, most Afghans didn't have it so good. A large majority of them lived on very little. Everyone had his hand out trying to get into my pockets. I felt guilty walking down the street when an old man begged me for backsheesh—just a small amount of money to help a beggar get by and I kept going, ignoring his request. I didn't bring so much money on my trip that I could afford to keep giving it away. Still, I didn't feel good about it.

Poverty was everywhere. I walked by a woman holding her baby in her arms, the infant's tiny hand outstretched in my direction. It didn't take long for a child to learn. My stomach turned. I relented and gave the woman a couple of afghani coins. Another day, a boy followed me for several blocks back to my hotel. Along the way, two others joined him. All three called out to me again and again, "Backsheesh, meester. Backsheesh," until I arrived at my hotel. Being surrounded by so much hardship and scarcity was very difficult. But it also strengthened my resolve to work to make people's lives better in whatever way I could. I knew I would be going home at some point, and there would be plenty to do in that regard in Nixon's America.

In the meantime, I wrote my folks another letter before I left Kabul. After bringing them up to date on where I had been and what I was doing, I again tried to explain how I felt. I told them I was restless and discontented and that I was trying to work it out, but it wasn't easy. I knew they thought I should come home, get a job, and try working it out that way. I pointed out that it would be difficult to look for a job when I didn't know what I wanted to do and didn't want just any job. If I had spent more time in the past just being instead of always working to become something, rushing toward uncertain goals that I never actually desired, perhaps I would be more sure of myself today, I admitted.

I was uncertain about my future but felt it would be more secure if I lived in the present. A job wasn't going to give me that security. It had to come from within. I told them that was what my trip was all about.

I mailed my letter with some hesitation, knowing my parents didn't want to know about my insecurity or that I wasn't yet ready to come home. The next day I prepared to leave Kabul alone. Ginger and I hadn't been getting along for weeks. While we had been traveling together for close to two months since leaving Tehran, it was more for convenience than any true friendship or fondness for each other. There were no hard feelings. It was just time for us to go our separate ways. More than anything, I was relieved. No more hassles or mixed messages.

I caught the overnight train that would whisk me through the entire Pakistani countryside. Once again, I was on my own on the road to India, the promised land.

9

ARRIVING IN INDIA, THE PROMISED LAND

MORE THAN SIX MONTHS AFTER leaving the States, I arrived in India the last week of November. While I didn't know what to expect, I felt that just getting there was a worthy accomplishment. Even my hungry ghost was a bit satisfied, though it still craved for much more.

I joined thousands of others from around the globe going to India in the late 1960s and much of the '70s. Many were in search of a guru and spiritual guidance. They were following in the footsteps of Harvard professor Ricard Alpert, who went there in 1967 and met his Hindu yogi, Neem Karoli Baba. Alpert received the name Ram Dass, Servant of God, from Baba and became his disciple. After returning to America, Ram Dass wrote *Be Here Now*, which popularized Eastern spirituality and helped make India a desirable destination for many who were dissatisfied with modern Western culture.

Others were called to India by the Beatles. Early in 1968, they traveled there as well. Along with Ram Dass, their journey East generated tremendous interest in India among their millions of fans. India quickly became the place to go for spiritual seekers and New Age enthusiasts alike.

As for me, I really wasn't sure why I had traveled thousands of miles to India. Before I left the States, I was intrigued by my friends' Indian experiences, as well as Ram Dass's book. The Beatles' foray into Eastern music lured me too. I had become captivated by the mysticism of India, and I wanted to discover what that was all about.

My initial stop in India gave me a hint of what that might be. It was a promising beginning to my time there. At first, I had no idea why the streets of Amritsar were so mobbed. But I soon learned that I had arrived on a very propitious occasion, the celebration of Guru Nanak's 503rd birthday at the spectacular Golden Temple, the holiest shrine in the Sikh religion. Tens of thousands of Sikh pilgrims from all over the world had come to the temple in reverence to Guru Nanak, the founder of Sikhism.

Though records indicated he was born on April 15, 1469, Guru Nanak's birth was celebrated on the November full moon. I later discovered that the November date was considered the time of his "spiritual birth," his enlightenment around the age of thirty. At that time, according to legend, Nanak heard the voice of God anointing him as a Guru and instructing him that the prevailing Muslim-Hindu religious dichotomy was null and void. He then proclaimed the unified oneness of God.

I felt lucky to be at the Golden Temple at such an auspicious time. It was the biggest birthday bash I'd ever attended. All day long, Sikhs and nonbelievers like me lined up to enter the Golden Temple to pay homage to Guru Nanak. Everyone—regardless of caste, sect, sex, or religion—was welcome, free of charge, in honor of Guru Nanak and his message of equality, fraternal love, and goodness. Not only was I inspired by the Sikhs' profound reverence for their founding guru, but my hungry ghost also received some potent nourishment as well. Deep inside, I could feel something awakening in me, an energy I had rarely known in my life.

The Golden Temple shimmered in the center of a large, man-made pool. Its gold-plated dome sat atop the main shrine, decorated with intricate designs and surrounded by smaller domes and minarets. I was astonished by the overly ornate architecture and again found myself wondering why the human race went to such costly extremes to pay tribute to its religious icons while providing so little to uplift the poor and hungry, which practically all faiths called us to do. The extravagant Golden Temple was just another example of why so many people around the world had turned away from organized religion. I doubted Guru Nanak would have approved of such extravagance. I was sure that Jesus would not have supported the immense sums the Church has expended in his name either. While feeling dismayed and mystified, I still stayed in line to cross the walkway over the water and get a closer look at the magnificent sanctuary.

As I entered the Golden Temple, the aroma of jasmine incense filled the air with a heavenly scent. I was in awe of this exquisite structure filled with large bouquets of flowers. Unfortunately, I could not escape the moving line to better examine the ornate inner sanctum. Before I knew it, I was out the other side.

That night, stunning fireworks featuring a variety of shapes and colors lit the sky over the temple for hours. They were as good, if not better, than any I'd ever seen on the Fourth of July back home. Dazzled by the wonderful light show, I could hardly believe I had unknowingly arrived in Amritsar just in time to catch this Sikh extravaganza. I was starting to realize that I did not have to know where I was going to get where I wanted to be: a place filled with history, beauty and spirit.

From Amritsar, I took a train to Agra, the home of the Taj Mahal, one of the seven wonders of the world. When I got off the train, I entered a large, dirt covered plaza filled with rickshaws, India's three-wheeled bicycle version of a taxi. Immediately, I was surrounded by drivers eager for me to hire them. A polite man who appeared to be around fifty caught my attention. I asked him to take me to see the Taj Mahal as I stepped into the back seat of his open rickshaw.

"My name is Rakesh," he said, introducing himself. "I would be happy to take you there. If you would like, I will take you around during your stay in Agra. What is your name? Where are you from?"

As Rakesh began peddling, I told him my name and that I was from New Jersey in the United States.

"I have a son, Manish, a little younger than you," he said. "I'm sure he would like to meet you. Would you come to my home and meet him after we go to the Taj Mahal?"

How could I pass up another opportunity to visit local people in their own homes? I knew it would enrich my journey as it had in England and Morocco, so I agreed. A short time later, we reached the entrance to the gardens surrounding the incredible monument.

"I will wait for you here while you explore the Taj," Rakesh said.

He was so friendly and polite that any suspicions I had concerning his motives melted away. At the same time, I was beginning to understand that he was taking me under his wing so he would have a steady customer for as long as I stayed in Agra. That was fine with me.

As I entered the walled grounds of the Taj Mahal, I felt I had stepped into another world, one like nothing I had ever seen before. I was stunned by its imposing beauty. While I had been impressed with the Golden Temple's ornate and intricate splendor, the Taj Mahal's dignified, ivory-white marbled eloquence far surpassed it. The interior was just as exquisite. The octagonal chamber of the mausoleum was inlaid with intricate designs containing thirty types of precious and semiprecious stones laid out in floral and abstract patterns. The stones came from all over Asia: jasper from Punjab, jade from China, turquoise from Tibet, lapis lazuli and sapphire from Sri Lanka, and white diamonds from Rajasthan.

Walking through its twenty-two magnificent chambers, I understood why the Taj Mahal was considered one of the seven wonders of the world. Built in the 1600s to house the tomb of the favorite wife of the Mughal emperor, Shah Jahan, the Taj Mahal clearly demonstrated how much he loved her. It was not just the structure itself, which appeared absolutely perfect. The pristine gardens and long, narrow reflection pool leading up to the Taj added another level of majesty to the heavenly atmosphere. I was so captivated by the Taj that later in my Indian adventure, I returned to immerse myself in its grandeur again.

When I finally pulled myself away from the Taj, Rakesh was waiting outside the gates just as he had promised. From there, he drove me to his home, a small concrete building with only three sides, the fourth being open to a small cement patio. The whole structure couldn't have been any bigger than my parents' one-car garage.

While that surprised me, what happened next floored me. "Would you like to stay here with me and my son, Manish, as our guest while you are in Agra?" Rakesh asked as he poured me a cup of chai. I couldn't believe he wanted to share his humble abode with me. While it didn't seem there was even enough room for Rakesh and his son, I could not refuse. "Here is where you will sleep," he said, pointing to his son's rough fiber cot in one corner of the room. Manish would stay next door at his friend's home while I was there.

When Manish came home from school, Rakesh introduced us. Bigger than his father, Manish was a good-looking seventeen-year-old with black hair and a strong body. Over a dinner of dal and lentils, Rakesh proudly explained that he had been a rickshaw driver for more than twenty years. He was now the head of the drivers' union, which consisted of three hundred men. Most drivers didn't own their rickshaws. They either rented them from the rickshaw company or were employees of the company. The union Rakesh led bargained with the company over rental fees, salaries, and working conditions.

It had been a full day, and I was tired. So after dinner, I thanked Rakesh and went to bed feeling extremely grateful for how well and effortlessly my Agra adventure was unfolding. While I lay in bed that night, I again marveled at how those like Rakesh, who had so little, were freely willing to share what they had. Yet a fair number of those who had a great deal were not so generous. It was very puzzling to me until I realized that when you have little, sharing is a way of developing mutual support and community. On the other hand, some of the wealthy who were less willing to share withdrew and lived in gated communities to protect themselves and their wealth from the rest of society. It seemed to me that it was one of the biggest problems dividing people in their respective countries, as well as in the world.

The next day, Rakesh took me to a shop that sold soapstone pipes, bowls, Buddhas, and other items. They were all colorful and attractive. I assumed he had some arrangement with the owner for a commission on anything bought by the customers he brought to the shop. I liked what the owner showed me and decided to buy some pieces that might be popular back home. I was continuing to think import sales could be a good business for me in the States and talked to the owner about an arrangement where he would ship orders to me if the business materialized. As I thanked the owner, dreams of a successful enterprise bubbled up in my mind.

I was excited as I got ready to leave Agra the next day. My hungry ghost was feeling at least somewhat satisfied. My trip to Agra had been a great experience in a number of ways: my time at the incomparable Taj Mahal, making friends with Rakesh and Manish, and developing a potential business with the soapstone dealer. I didn't know how to thank Rakesh enough for his generous hospitality and for introducing me to the shop owner. As I was saying goodbye to Manish, it came to me. I put my hand in my pocket and pulled out my prized Swiss Army knife. From the smile on his face as I handed it to him,

I could see how much Manish appreciated it. We hugged and I wished him well in his studies. Then Rakesh took me back to the station to catch the next train to Varanasi—one of the seven sacred cities of Hinduism.

10

BEGINNING TO FIND PEACE

On the train to Varanasi, I made some new American friends, Barbara, Danielle, John, and Encke. While we all got to know each other during the twenty-hour train ride, Barbara asked me why I had come to India.

"In twenty-five words or less?" I responded lightheartedly.

"One word, if you can," she said, challenging me.

I hesitated for a minute, then replied in earnest, "Peace. Peace of mind is what I'm after." In that moment, I realized I'd said something that truly resonated with me. Whether I would find it remained to be seen, I admitted to myself. I didn't expect to turn a corner in Varanasi or Bombay and suddenly be enlightened. I knew that anyone who came to India with that notion would be sadly disappointed.

I understood that learning to be content could be a long, slow process—actually, more of a practice than a process. But did I really have to travel all the way to India to discover that? Still, I began to understand that it was the main reason I had left the States. After three hectic months in Europe, I hadn't come any closer to gaining peace of mind. So I had turned to the East and went to mystical India in search of it.

As those thoughts stirred in my mind, my body became more at ease. I felt softer, more relaxed, quieter. Slowly, I began delving into the real source of the problem: my mind. What was I really all about? Who was the being underneath all the outer layers? At the core, I wanted to know the real me and become comfortable in my being. Finally, I was on to something. At last I had gotten a clearer sense of what I was looking for.

The five of us decided to get a place together in Varanasi. We started out sharing a room in the Central Hotel. Five in a room was tight, but it turned out to be an arrangement that helped bring us closer together.

John was a real character, clever and quick on his feet. "Seeded rolls. When you come to Brooklyn, I promise to take you for seeded rolls," he said as he handed me an unseeded piece of Indian flatbread called chapati. An easygoing, bearded hippie from Brooklyn, John then magically pulled a die out of his ear. I thought he was a bit crazy, but he was fun to be around.

That got the good times rolling. Barbara picked up her guitar and began strumming. John improvised a song while Barbara shouted out one of her own, overtaking John's verse. "And from the people who live in the steeple, we have a message for you," John sang as he pictured us in a steeple on top of the hotel.

"Good evening, ladies and gentlemen. Channel 29 proudly brings you *The Autobiography of a Yogi*, but first…" I pretended to announce an imaginary TV show, reflecting all the zaniness in the room. My hungry ghost didn't have a clue of what to make of it all and just disappeared.

Barbara stopped playing and picked up my copy of *The Autobiography of a Yogi*, opened it randomly, and read a paragraph imploring everyone to focus on living fully in the present. It reminded me of Ram Dass's *Be Here Now*. Then she broke into another driving melody, singing, "Where we gonna be for Christmas, Lord?"

Encke chimed in. "It's less than three weeks away."

John relit his hash-filled chillum, a popular conical Indian smoking pipe. We were all pretty high by then and having a blast.

Meanwhile, Danielle was getting a massage on my bed from a happy little Indian man with a long, curled mustache. She was blissed out. The Indian smiled, really digging it too. He cracked her knuckles. Then he gave her a bear hug with his knees in her back and his hands folded across her breasts. One by one, John, Encke, Barbara, and I each got worked on by the little Indian man. Under his superb hands, I floated into a dreamy realm while the rest of the troop sang, "Ji Baba, Ji Baba! Praise to Ji Baba! He's our man!"

Babaji was considered a deathless avatar. While I knew nothing about him, we all hailed him as the great being who delivered us into our stoned state of ecstasy.

In addition to the wild times we were having, there was a totally different focal point to my time in Varanasi, the ancient traditions of the Hindus. One of the world's oldest, continually inhabited cities, dating back over twenty-five hundred years, Varanasi was renowned for its many ghats. Situated alongside the Ganges River, these platforms were where the Hindus cremated their dead.

One day I walked along the river and watched as numerous people stepped from the stone slabs of the ghats into the muddy waters of the holy river to cleanse themselves and wash their clothes. Since they were being spiritually purified, it didn't seem to matter to them that they were bathing in water that was quite dirty.

Later, I saw a group of mourners at another ghat place the body of a deceased man on a large, wooden funeral pyre that was about four feet high. They chanted hymns as they lit the wood and cremated the body. According to Hindu tradition, the fire released the soul from the body and washed away its sins. There were bodies burning on several other ghats, which filled the air with black smoke. The sickening smell was subdued by sandalwood and other incense. I had a difficult time absorbing this strange, holy scene into my Western way of thinking, but as I walked back to the hotel, a sense of reverence filled my soul. My hungry ghost had taken in something it had never encountered before and didn't quite know what to make of it.

After the intensity of the burning ghats, I was glad to return to my little band of merrymakers at the hotel and get stoned. Like me, Encke had been traveling alone before meeting up with the others on the train. He was a tall, laid-backed fellow from Texas with a little bit of a twang in his voice. Encke also had a kilo of Afghan hash he was planning to sell when he got to Goa, where he was sure he could get more for it. But he was running out of rupees, so he quickly became the local dealer for the hippie community living around Benares Hindi University. It really seemed out of character for him. Encke was kind of quiet and unassertive, not the drug dealer type in my mind.

After a few days in a noisy hotel, we'd all had enough of the city and moved out to the university area. Barbara found a far-out little apartment across the road from the university in the suburban countryside outside Varanasi. It had a large tropical garden for a backyard we could view from our apartment balcony. At night we could go up on the roof and breathe in the wonder of the star-filled sky. It was so peaceful, almost heaven.

Our apartment became the gathering place for the new friends we were making. We met Michael from England in our Varanasi hotel. He and his Japanese buddy, Marbo, came with us to see the apartment Barbara had found. They decided to move to the university area as well. One day they dropped by with some fresh Afghan hash Marbo had picked up in Mazar. Verna, a wandering vagabond from Vienna, also came by. In the time it took to fill a chillum, we were all stoned again.

Verna started playing his flute. Michael got out his guitar and began strumming. Then Barbara picked up her guitar and joined in. Feet were tapping, fingers were snapping, and John was boogying. We ate peanuts, drank tea, rapped, smoked, and made music for hours.

Besides making music and smoking, evening feasts were our favorite activity, the hedonistic climax to our fun-filled festive life. We were continually buying, preparing, and devouring food. Our dinners usually consisted of rice, beans, and a variety of fresh vegetables, often followed by tea and a dessert of fruit and curd. Still, we weren't averse to Colonel Sanders' fried chicken and a six-pack of Coors on occasion. For breakfast, we had fruit-filled pancakes and curd or French toast with fresh cinnamon. And we always had tea, fresh oranges, and bananas. John took charge of the kitchen. A four-year Navy vet, he made sure everything was kept shipshape.

After several days of hanging out in our little paradise, Barbara and Danielle came back from a morning in Varanasi.

"We got in, we got in," they yelled gleefully. Then they explained that we could all take the ten-day Vipassana meditation course they had just signed up for, taught by Goenka, a highly regarded Burmese meditation teacher.

Unfortunately, the course started that same evening. We had just moved in and unpacked a few days earlier and now our lady friends wanted us to pack up and move again. John, Encke, and I immediately decided we weren't going anywhere, so Barbara and Danielle got their stuff together and took off for the course. The three of us put our feet up and relaxed. It felt great. We had more space to spread out and more peace and quiet in which to enjoy our serene surroundings.

A couple of days later, I was sitting in the garden surrounded by lush palm and papaya trees, their leaves swaying in the breeze. Purple and white snowball blossoms danced next to me. Birds chirped in the distance. Two cotton clouds provided a soft bed for the half-moon visible in the late afternoon sky. I began reflecting on how lucky I was to be living in this beautiful place in true harmony with two other guys. Each of us was willing to do our share of what needed to get done without any hassles. Friends dropped in to chat, smoke, and play music. The food was delicious. Life was very good. I wondered what more I could want, ignoring the hungry ghost still lurking inside me.

Then suddenly that ghost popped up again, not letting me enjoy the simple, easy life I was living. Thoughts of faraway family and friends as well as buried desires of finding fulfilling work and lasting love pulled me away from my Garden of Eden ecstasy. I could not escape those haunting thoughts and feelings. Plus, the owner of the apartment would soon be returning to reclaim her space, and we would have to leave our lovely refuge.

A few days later, Encke and I bade farewell to John and our delightful garden as we prepared to board a two-day train to Bombay (more recently known as Mumbai). While sad to leave, we were sure there would be more good times to come. When I was on the road from Istanbul to Kabul, I had heard "Goa for Christmas! Goa for Christmas!" again and again from fellow travelers. It must be an amazing place, I thought, since everyone I ran into was going there. Encke and I figured we could get to Bombay just in time to make the Christmas Eve boat and arrive in Goa Christmas morning.

The train was mobbed. It reminded me of the one from Fez, so crowded we had to jump out the window to get off. Since we would be riding for two days and didn't have a sleeper compartment, I climbed up on the wooden luggage rack above the seats, stretched out, and made myself a semi-comfortable bed. Traveling third class, unreserved, I quickly learned how to improvise. It sure beat standing up in the aisle for two days.

"Bring on the dancing girls," I wrote in my journal as we waited for the ferry on the dock in Bombay. From what I'd gathered, Goa was one big party, and I was more than ready to party. Goa had been on my mind for some time. Now I would be arriving there on Christmas day, just like those travelers I'd met along the way. It was a long boat ride, around eighteen hours. When I wasn't dozing off, I spent the time reflecting on my trip in my journal, noting, among other things, that there was a natural course of events.

I look out and a path appears in front of me. Effortlessly, I follow it. I'm beginning to think that there is 'a way out of here.' All I have to do is go with the flow, like the mellow Ganges on a lazy afternoon. Things really do take care of themselves if you just let them.

The sun was just taking its nightly dip into the Indian Ocean. Streaks of clouds stretched out from the pool of light left behind by the setting sun. The arms of the universe, those wispy clouds, gently ushered in the darkness like a mother covering her sleeping child with a blanket. As lyrics from "Truckin'" by the Grateful Dead played in my head, I thought about "what a long, strange trip it's been." Half asleep on the deck of the ferry to Goa, I sensed that something quite remarkable was happening. I was riding the cosmic energy guiding me to the state of peace of mind I'd unknowingly been seeking my entire journey. My hungry ghost was aroused. I could feel it in my bones.

11

WANDERING IN PARADISE

I STEPPED OFF THE BOAT and onto the glistening, golden beaches of Goa Christmas morning. Immediately, I got why the Western vagabonds I'd met traveling overland to India were all invoking "Goa for Christmas! Goa for Christmas!" And I had made it right on time. It was love at first sight.

Though Goa was part of the Indian subcontinent, it felt like an island paradise to me. I had a thing for islands. There was something about being surrounded by water, cut off from all the hubbub and tumult of the mainland, that I found stimulating. With the ocean breeze blowing through my hair, I felt full of life with a boundless sense of freedom.

Though not an island, Goa inspired me in that same way. The aqua-blue ocean was as clear as the swimming pool at my parents' country club. The pristine beaches were bordered by a forest of majestic palm trees with broad, green leaves that reached out to greet me. With just a few bamboo fruit stands, the tranquil beaches reminded me of simpler, more primitive times.

About 250 miles south of Bombay, Goa was unlike the rest of Hindu India. Formerly a Portuguese possession with a strong Catholic presence, the province did not become part of India until 1962. In addition to its island-like atmosphere, a Western religious heritage made Goa unique. Putting all those qualities together created an area very different from any other part of India I'd experienced. There weren't the hundreds of rickshaw drivers hustling me to hire them as my guide. Nor were there hungry Indian children pulling at my heartstrings, always begging for backsheesh. Nor the street noise and busy crowds of Indian cities. Goa was far removed from all that, undemanding, peaceful, and beautiful. My hungry ghost was completely at ease.

Soon after we landed, Encke and I parted. While he wanted to stay put and just soak up the sun and sand, I decided to meander up the beach. Besides, he still had a good deal of that Afghan hash to sell and needed to set up shop in one place where potential customers could find him.

"Goodbye, Encke. It's been great traveling with you," I said as I lifted my pack onto my back, preparing to head up the beach.

"Good luck, my friend. I've really enjoyed our time together," Encke replied as we hugged. "I hope we will meet again in the States someday."

With that, I turned and began strolling toward the next episode in my uncharted journey.

A couple of days later, I arrived at Calangute Beach. Hungry, I walked up to a food shack at the edge of the beach to get some lunch. As I put my pack down, I looked up and couldn't believe who was standing in front of me. With a big smile on her face, there stood Lorrie, one of my VW bus traveling buddies.

"Hi, stranger," she said, greeting me. "When did you arrive?"

"Wow! What a surprise!" I replied in amazement. "I got here Christmas morning. And you?"

"We've been here for more than a month now. We rented a nice little place on the beach just a short way from here. Why don't you come up and see everyone?"

Still shaking my head in disbelief, I followed Lorrie to a simple, white stucco house with the old VW van parked outside. Lorrie opened the door and announced, "Look who I found."

Mac, Toad, and Mindy all turned toward us and were startled to see me.

"Well, I'll be," Mac declared. "Come on in and take a load off. Want something to drink?"

I thanked him and noted how relaxed he seemed. I could tell beach life agreed with him.

"Hi! Man!" Toad said while Mindy managed a friendly smile.

For the next couple of hours, we exchanged stories of our adventures since we parted in Mashhad. I told them the stirring story of my incredible trip from Herat to Mazar-i-Sharif, which had them on the edge of their seats. Of course, they asked about Ginger.

"Well, we barely managed to keep traveling together until we got to Kabul. By then, we were both more than glad to go our separate ways. I haven't seen her since."

Mac lit a fat joint and passed it around. He and Lorrie shared how they drove from Afghanistan to India and down to Goa with only one minor glitch. They were detained at the Pakistani border for several hours while the customs agents did a very thorough search of their minibus. Fortunately, the agents didn't find any contraband and eventually let them through.

"So what are your plans now?" Mac asked after a while.

"Just moseying up the beach. That's as much as I know at this point."

Mac glanced at Lorrie, who nodded her approval. "Well, you're welcome to stay here for a while."

Caught by surprise, I thought for a moment and said, "That'd be great. Really appreciate it. What an unexpected turn of events."

Goa offered plenty of time and space to clean out my mind and gain a clearer perspective of the world and myself. I'd been searching for a place like Goa for a long time. That night I reflected on my travels in a letter to my sister, Bobbe, and her husband, Dick:

> It's strange, but the East really does contain quite a bit of magic and mysticism. There are a lot of holy people walking around here and they seem to have found some of the answers to life. Somehow the message seems to be getting communicated. Everybody discovers it for themselves in their own way. I think the atmosphere of the East must be more conducive to spiritual communication. Or maybe the people who come here are more ready to receive the message than those who remain in the West. Nonetheless, something is definitely happening here, and a lot of people are being affected by it.
>
> Love, Bruce

Two days later was New Year's Eve. That morning, I roamed down to a secluded rock ledge on Calangute Beach overlooking the ocean. I took out an Indian aerogramme and began writing to my folks. After wishing them a happy New Year, I attempted to convey from my heart how much my traveling experience meant to me. I was dying for them to understand how valuable it was. I told them I had come to Goa to bathe in its tranquility and soothing waters. "You realize, I'm sure, that everyone must seek peace for himself. Often it is a lonely and difficult journey, but those who persevere are richly rewarded. I believe that I have been rewarded. The experiences I have had and the knowledge that I have gained are priceless to me."

I assured them that there was no need for them to be unhappy or disturbed about my journey and that it was good for me. I asked them to have faith that all would turn out well and that it would be a very good new year for us all.

As I sealed the letter, I doubted my folks would actually grasp the value of what I was doing. From their perspective, I was a lost soul, and they had failed in their parental responsibility to instill in me the values of hard work and perseverance. If they had succeeded, I would be on the straight and narrow, middle-class path they were familiar with. While I was concerned about their feelings, I wasn't about to allow that to rob me of my newfound peace of mind.

At that moment, I would not even allow my hungry ghost, always grasping for more, to prevent me from basking in the sun and relaxing in my peace of mind. At the same time, I did feel just a little guilty. After all, my parents had paid my way through college and law school. They expected me to be making my way in the world as a practicing lawyer rather than as an unemployed drifter on the other side of the planet. While

I understood that, I knew this was what I had to do. I could not let their anxieties and desires deter me from my search for myself. I could only hope that someday, they would come to terms with how I chose to live my life.

Later that afternoon, as the sun began to set on the year 1972, I returned to that same rocky ledge to meditate. With the waves splashing against the nearby rocks, I sat naked in silent meditation. As I concentrated on my breath, I felt my body in harmony with the ocean waves and the sea breeze. I sensed my being merging with the planetary vibrations as though I were making love to the universe. In my altered state, my hungry ghost was sleeping peacefully, and I was filled with pure love, like nothing I had ever experienced before.

After a couple of blissful weeks hanging out on the beach, I packed my things and prepared to continue my wandering. I thanked my old traveling buddies for their generous hospitality, wished them the best, and once again, I was off. Just a short trek north, Anjuna Beach was my next destination. To get there, I had to take off my boots and carry my pack over my head as I crossed a fairly shallow river that flowed into the Arabian Sea. In a matter of hours, I was on Anjuna Beach, the epicenter of the hippie movement in India.

Anjuna was a tiny village among the rice fields and coconut palms just off the beach. Perfectly lined with giant palms, it was perhaps the most beautiful beach I'd ever been to. In my mind, Anjuna was India's mini version of Woodstock, absent the rock stars. Hundreds of long hairs and flower children were spread out over the sun-soaked beach. Some put up tents or makeshift huts. Many others, like me, just slept on a blanket or in their sleeping bags. In the evenings, campfires dotted the beach, each circled by twenty or so ramblers from Australia,

Europe, the States, and other far-off places. We sang, ate, drank, smoked, and told stories. As the light of the moon grew, some of us took a dip in the sea.

The night of the full moon was a particularly special time. Lively music roared from giant speakers on the beach. I heard that Peter Townshend and his band, The Who, had donated them just for the occasion. I could tell it was going to be quite an event. Over two hundred hippies had gathered for the beach party. Though I hardly knew anyone, it felt like we were all one big, happy family. Bonfires lit the beach, the aroma of pot filled the air, rock music galvanized the crowd, and half-naked bodies danced joyfully. The peak of my Goa experience, that full moon bash, was an unforgettable night.

Like most of the hippies and seekers I met in Anjuna, Goa was only a temporary resting ground. By the end of January, I was ready to continue my journey. As I was preparing to leave, I wrote my sister and brother-in-law, telling them I was heading to Nepal and the Himalayas, continuing my search for knowledge. "Who knows, I might even come across a Tibetan Buddhist monk and find enlightenment," I wrote. "Then my wandering soul should be ready to return home."

I shared that one of the things I'd discovered was that we can have whatever we want if we have the will to obtain it. "The more you direct your thoughts and your energies toward that which you desire, the more easily you will realize those wishes." I told them I believed good thoughts led to good actions.

I must have been pretty high when I wrote that, but all the seekers and hippies in Goa were living proof that a different way of life was possible. Some might say, I was "drinking the Kool-Aid." Still, I felt the atmosphere in Goa was infused with that vibe. Then again, I wondered whether we were all just in some temporary, incredible bubble removed from the real world. Could we actually take this New Age thinking back home and transform society? While I left Goa inspired, I wasn't quite ready to confront these very challenging questions.

What I experienced in Goa was a very special life of simple pleasures. Some people knew that the Western world could never provide that and refused to return home. That was not for me. As much as I loved hanging out on the beach and getting high, I knew I could not reject my life in America. My family and friendship ties were too strong. And I wanted to do my part in making my country a better place for everyone.

It became clear to me that my desire for a life of meaning and purpose was what was driving my hungry ghost. I knew that living in Goa would not offer me the opportunity to create such a life. What could was still a mystery to me.

12

DISCOVERING BUDDHISM

I GOT EXCITING NEWS WHEN I picked up my mail in Bombay after I left Goa the first week in February. My cousin Eddie was getting married the beginning of April. Since I planned to return to the States in the spring anyway, I decided to surprise everyone and come home in time to attend the wedding.

Air India had a once-a-week, nonstop flight from Delhi to Amsterdam. I immediately booked it for the latter part of March and also scheduled my return flight from Amsterdam to New York.

Suddenly, my journey was reduced to just six more weeks, and I still had much ground to cover. At that point, hiking in the Himalayas was my number one priority. Several people had told me about the spectacular trek from Pokhara, Nepal, at 2700 feet to the Annapurna Base Camp at an altitude of 13,550 feet. Round trip, the trek would take nine or ten days.

From Pokhara back to Delhi would be another three days. I first had to get from Bombay to Kathmandu, a distance of over 1250 miles, then to Pokhara. Combined, that would take several days as well.

But there was one stop I had to make on my way to Kathmandu. Bodh Gaya was considered to be the holiest site in Buddhism. It was said that Prince Siddhartha became enlightened, attaining Buddhahood, in 589 BC beneath the Bodhi tree, the tree of awakening, in that small village. Just 154 miles east of Varanasi, I couldn't pass up a visit to Bodh Gaya.

While I had no prior knowledge or involvement in Buddhism, my intuition drew me to that sacred place. The entire village was filled with ancient, medieval, and modern shrines, monasteries, and temples. I could not help but be moved by the spiritual vibration that permeated the village.

Though the original Bodhi tree was no longer living, a replica said to be a direct descendant of the original, stood in its place. As I approached this hallowed ground, awe and reverence filled my being. How could I be so taken by something I knew nothing about? Whatever had come over me, I felt a strong connection to Buddhism.

Buddhism was unique among the world's major religions because it didn't address the question of whether God exists. In fact, many considered Buddhism a philosophy of life, a way of being in the world, rather than a religion. Its focus was on exploring how we think, feel, and act. It investigated the nature of reality, ending suffering, and achieving enlightenment. That seemed like a path to becoming happier, which sounded good to me.

The Buddhist concept that most deeply resonated with me was that we are all one, interconnected and interdependent. If we were all one, then whatever I did affected everyone else and vice versa. That made human beings one big universal family. According to Buddhist teachings, we were all integral parts of one universe sharing one energy field or one consciousness. It made a lot of sense to me. Ironically, science was coming to the same conclusion. Quantum mechanics posited that everything was connected, just like the Buddha taught. It found that the universe was made up of interconnected, unified space in constant communication, where distance and time were of no consequence. And one end of the universe moved in synch with and in relationship to the other end.

But how did this all come about? Western religions turned to God as the answer. Science proposed the big bang theory, which hypothesized that the universe started with a dense single point that inflated and stretched.

Buddhism posited that there is no beginning or end to the universe. Accordingly, time is infinite. Therefore, there is no need to suppose a supreme being created the universe. That made more sense to me than the existence of a god overseeing the universe.

Having grown up in the Jewish faith, I was taught that God did exist. Yet it was never clear to me what or who God was. In fact, Judaism taught that God was beyond human comprehension. Still, I had a hard time believing in a supreme being who created the universe. Buddhism provided a reasonable alternative.

Going to Bodh Gaya whetted my appetite for exploring Buddhism more. The town felt like one interconnected holy land with temples representing Chinese, Japanese, Bhutanese, and Thai Buddhist traditions, among others. But I had no time to visit any of them. The Himalayas were calling me. Still, my little taste of Buddhism prompted a second stop on my way to Nepal. Just seven miles northeast of Varanasi was Sarnath, another of the four most important Buddhist pilgrimage destinations. It had special significance because it was there in Deer Park that the Buddha gave his first sermon after attaining enlightenment. In that discourse, the Buddha formulated what came to be known as the Four Noble Truths, the foundation of Buddhist teachings.

My mind was swirling by the time I left Sarnath. While I was not ready to give up all my traditional Jewish beliefs to embrace Buddhism, I could not disregard all the new ideas and principles I discovered in my tour of Deer Park and the literature I gathered there. Still, it would take a great deal of meditation and study for this Buddhist seed that had been planted in my being to sprout and flourish.

At the same time, I again remembered the evening I had spent with my former girlfriend and her husband during which they referred to the secrets of India I would have to discover for myself. While I had just scratched the surface, I was beginning to grasp what they meant. Beneath all the poverty and chaos, I realized that India held centuries of spiritual treasures.

A whole new world was opening up to me. But I had more immediate marvels to explore. With less than two months to go on my journey, I turned my thoughts and attention to getting to Nepal and the wonder of trekking in the Himalayas, the highest mountain range in the world.

13

ALLOWING THE UNIVERSE TO LEAD THE WAY

WHILE RIDING ON THE ROOF of a large truck's cab with two fellow travelers, I was ecstatic as the majestic Himalayas came into view. Surrounded by the world's highest, snowcapped mountains under big blue skies left me breathless as we entered the Kathmandu valley. But everything turned upside down once we arrived in Nepal's capital city.

As soon as I got settled in my hotel room, I headed for the post office. One of my first stops whenever I got to a city was always the post office or whatever mail delivery location I had given people. Hearing from back home always made my day. Traveling alone for the most part, I relished receiving letters connecting me with friends and family from halfway around the world.

On March 9, I eagerly opened an aerogramme from my sister Bobbe outside the Kathmandu post office. What I read broke my heart. My Aunt Ida Berlin, cousin Eddie's mom, had died of a massive heart attack. Bobbe wrote that my father was quite upset at the funeral. "If it was one of us, my son wouldn't even know," he'd said sadly. She asked if I was still alive since they had not heard from me in two months and urged me to write and let them know I was okay. I hadn't realized it had been that long since I'd written anyone.

Tears filled my eyes. I couldn't believe it. My Aunt Ida was in her fifties. Way too young to die, I thought. I admired her. In my mind, she was the perfect mother, always attentive to her son's needs and desires.

My cousin Eddie and I were quite close. At only twenty-six, he had just lost the person he most counted on his whole life. I wrote Eddie how deeply sorry and heartbroken I was. I didn't know what else to say. On top of that, I had recently received a letter from him telling me that he and his fiancée, Phyllis, had broken up. He wrote that their April wedding was off, so there was no need to rush home. To make matters even worse, he explained that he hated his job. I felt very sad for my good friend, but there was really nothing I could do from so far away.

At the same time, I had to cope with my dad's angst over thinking I would not have been there if he or my mom had been the one to have fallen ill and died. That was in addition to grappling with Dad's severe displeasure with my choices. He had written me about how unhappy and disturbed he and my mother were regarding my being halfway around the world.

Dad's letter weighed heavily on my heart. I so much wanted him to understand what I was going through and why I needed to take this extended journey far from home. I wrote back trying my best to get him to see the value of my travels:

Dear Mom and Dad,

What you as parents and builders of the great American society fail to see is that your children, the next generation, have a different role to play. You have done your part; we must and will do ours.

If the society is to evolve upward, if there is to be real progress, we, the offspring of the affluent society, cannot imitate you. That would lead to stagnation, not progress. Rather, we must go out on our own and discover new paths which will bring man closer to his true being and to the professed ideals of our society. And that's exactly what is happening. We have come to India in search of the evolutionary path.

History is unfolding and we are playing our part. Your generation can be proud of the part you played, the sacrifices of world wars and depression and the creation of a post-war nation. Broaden your perspective and just be a little patient and I'm certain that you will also be able to take pride in me and the achievements of my generation. As Prime Minister Trudeau of Canada said when he was informed that he had been returned to power by a one-seat margin in parliament, in the universal cosmic order, everything is occurring as it should.

So please don't be disturbed and disappointed, Mom and Dad. You can still have faith in yourselves as parents and much hope for the future of your children. For I have great faith that one day soon you shall come to realize the true value of my journey....

All my love,
Your son,
Bruce

"You have become quite a philosopher," Dad replied. "It's pretty hard to appreciate what you're thinking from our position back here. However, we should have a lot to talk about when you get back."

I felt I was finally getting through to my father, at least to some degree, and gained renewed hope for the future of our relationship.

Still, I was confused and didn't know what to do. I thought about rushing back to the States to alleviate my parents' agony and support Eddie in his grieving. But I doubted how much help I could really provide. And I only had two months to go before my roundtrip ticket back to New York expired, so I would be returning then anyhow. I seriously contemplated exchanging my March ticket to Amsterdam for a flight in May so I could fulfill my dream of trekking in the Himalayas.

The next day, the universe gave me a clue about what direction to take with the sudden appearance of a third option. I was walking down the street in Kathmandu when I saw a couple I recognized from my days at NYU Law School. While I didn't know them, Lynda and Lenny had been in several of my classes. Lynda was unmistakable, a strikingly attractive woman with long black hair and an inviting smile. I couldn't believe I was bumping into my former classmates in this remote place so far from New York. I immediately went up to them and introduced myself. They were as surprised as me to run into someone from NYU on the other side of the world.

"What are you doing here?" I asked.

"We're taking a month-long Tibetan Buddhist retreat at Kopan Monastery, not far from here," Lynda replied. Lenny explained the retreat would be facilitated by a Tibetan Rinpoche and would start in about a week.

"Wow!" I exclaimed. "That sounds amazing. I'm about to go trekking for a few days before I head to Delhi to catch my flight back to Amsterdam." I then told them how my visits to Bodh Gaya and Sarnath had sparked a newfound interest in Buddhism. As we parted, I wondered if it was somehow possible for me to change my plans and enroll in the Buddhist retreat at Kopan. That night I imagined how I could delay my departure, and participate in the retreat, and still get back to Amsterdam in time to catch a plane home before my ticket expired.

The next morning, I was shaken from my sleep when my whole room began to tremble. An earthquake had struck Kathmandu. The quake only lasted a few seconds, and fortunately, Kathmandu suffered little damage. But I sensed it was a wake-up call from the universe. Lynda and Lenny were divine messengers pointing me in the right direction.

The universe was also telling me it was time I shook up my world. I still had lessons to learn. My hungry ghost was far from satisfied. I was searching for meaning and yearning to find my true self. Who was I? What was my life all about? I couldn't go home until I had some answers.

I decided to do whatever I could to stay in Nepal and participate in the retreat at Kopan. Maybe this was what my hungry ghost had been seeking all along. So I went down to the Air India office to see if I could change my flight to Amsterdam to a date in the first half of May. Much to my disappointment, the airline's weekly flight to Amsterdam was all booked for the next few months. But I was determined. For the next several days, I went to the airline office and got the same result.

Then, on the last day before I was going to leave for Pokhara to begin my trek, a miracle occurred. Someone's plans had changed, and Air India now had an open seat on a flight to Amsterdam the second week of May. The universe had once again come through for me. What else could it be but divine intervention? I felt blessed.

I had no idea what I was getting into when I began the hot, forty-five-minute walk from Kathmandu to Kopan Monastery. Founded by Lama Yeshe and Thupten Zopa Rinpoche in 1969, the monastery consisted of one meditation temple on Kopan hill, at the base of which were small huts where the kitchen staff, monks, and students lived. The temple, the Nepal Buddhist Mahayana Center Gompa, had just been completed the previous year.

Lama Yeshe and Zopa Rinpoche had fled Tibet in 1959 following the Chinese invasion of their country. While horrific for the Tibetans, the invasion turned out to be a gift of sorts to the Western world. It was the impetus for the spread of Tibetan Buddhism to millions of people in the West.

Yeshe, the elder of the two lamas, directed the Kopan monastery. His vision was to create a center for the study and practice of Tibetan Buddhism for foreign students, as well as for young Himalayan monks. He hoped the center would inspire individuals with a good heart and noble wisdom to spread the dharma and serve others all over the world.

Yeshe and Rinpoche began giving dharma talks to mainly Western students who had heard about these extraordinary lamas. The first one-month meditation course was held in the spring of 1971. Twenty-five students attended. A year later, double that number enrolled. By the spring of 1973, a hundred students were attending each of the twice-yearly, one-month courses. We slept on the floor on straw mats. Our water supply depended on a local spring, and our food was carried up the hill by porters. My uneasiness entering the mysterious world of Tibetan Buddhism was somewhat lessened by my new connection with Lynda and Lenny. I didn't feel so alone. The universe had not only arranged my karma to bring me to this transformative retreat, it also provided some companions to support me in this totally unfamiliar venue.

Many foreigners, disillusioned with the increased materialistic outlook in the West, were looking for greater meaning in their lives. They flocked to Kopan to attend the lamas' teachings. I was about to become one of them.

14

LEARNING THE WAY OF THE BUDDHA

AFTER TEN MONTHS ON THE road, my travels were now taking me on a completely different kind of journey. Instead of exploring more of the wonders of the world, I was about to spend a month examining my inner being. I sensed it would be as challenging a time as I had ever experienced.

I was filled with nervous anticipation my first day at Kopan as I sat on my meditation cushion along with a hundred other spiritual seekers from all over the planet. I was about to enter the realm of Tibetan Buddhism for the first time.

When our teacher, Thubten Zopa Rinpoche, entered the large hall, we all rose, not so much to honor him but out of respect for the wisdom he embraced. When Zopa sat down on the dais in front of us, people began doing prostrations.

They got down on their knees three times and bent forward till their foreheads touched the floor in front of them each time. I followed their lead and began prostrating. While I felt a little awkward, I thought it was appropriate for me to go along with it, and I later learned it was a time-honored Buddhist tradition.

Thubten Zopa Rinpoche was a reincarnated lama in the Tibetan Gelug lineage. Rinpoche is the title given to all reincarnated lamas or teachers. He was a few years younger than me, and he looked it. Appearing rather humble, Zopa had a slim, frail-looking body and a boyish smile. He was dressed in traditional maroon Buddhist robes. Much to my surprise, he spoke in somewhat broken English.

He began by asking, "Why learn the Dharma?" And then he offered this answer: "All beings are conditioned by suffering. Rebirth, old age, disease, and death—all stages of life are suffering. From conception, one has no choice but to get older, which is suffering. There are many kinds of suffering. Dissatisfaction is the worst kind, a feeling that something is missing. Attachment and spending one's whole life supporting and making the body comfortable are also suffering. Ignorance—not recognizing the nature of the mind—is the source of all suffering. The three negative minds—greed, ignorance, and hatred—are the causes of all suffering. Achievement of real peace depends on your method. The dharma is the way."

I wasn't quite sure I got everything he said. But I knew I had come to the right place when Rinpoche explained that dissatisfaction was the worst kind of suffering. I felt he was talking directly to me as I reflected on the dissatisfaction I had experienced my entire trip. At the same time, my hungry ghost jumped to attention. What seemed clear to me was that from a Buddhist perspective, most of my life consisted of suffering.

Still, I didn't understand what Zopa meant by "the dharma." Was it the Buddhist teachings? Or the state of enlightenment? Or the understanding of the true nature of things? Or was it all three?

I slowly raised my hand. "Rinpoche, what do you mean by 'the dharma'?" I asked. "Can you define it, please?"

"Dharma is positive, pure mind and action," he replied. "Any action that helps to cut off the cause and results of suffering is dharma action. Understanding the mind is the door to dharma action and to happiness—enlightenment—which is the complete cessation of suffering."

I still didn't quite get it. But I decided I had to just keep listening and hope I would eventually understand what Zopa meant by the dharma. Then he switched gears and introduced a whole new concept that I had never heard of before.

"Mind is beginningless, continual, and impermanent. It is created by impulses. It depends on many conditions and is not independent. Mind never ends. It continues from one lifetime to the next effortlessly, flowing like a river through time. All form is a reflection according to the level of one's mind.

"The mind is like a mirror. Pure mind, enlightenment, is a clean mirror. We must clean the mind of negative conditioning and delusions to receive enlightenment. Ignorance is obscuration of the mind. We must eliminate ignorance through right understanding, making the mind one with the dharma, the purification of the mind."

I was beginning to see what Rinpoche was saying. The dharma was the Buddhist teaching that pure mind is enlightenment, which is achieved by eliminating suffering. But I wondered how we eliminated suffering. At the same time, I was struck by this young lama's grasp of the English language.

He used a word, "obscuration," that I had never used or had ever heard spoken before. That immediately raised my esteem for him.

I considered the morning discourse over lunch, a vegetarian meal the Tibetan kitchen staff served outside the *gompa*, a place of meditation and learning. The staff was unbelievable. Their every movement and gesture instantly displayed their dedication to serving us, complete strangers to them. One of the Tibetan staff poured me a glass of water with such gentle humility that it truly felt like an act of love. I was captivated by the Tibetans' simple, respectful demeanor. Their tender behavior toward us clearly demonstrated the value of living by the dharma.

I was also charmed by Lama Yeshe, the elder lama at Kopan. He had the broadest smile I had ever seen, and his eyes were filled with kindness. Short, plump, and jolly, he looked a bit like my image of Santa Claus. The dharma continuously flowed from him in gentle waves. Like all the attendees, I had two brief, private audiences with him during the retreat. When I met with him, he asked how I was doing and whether I had any questions, which I did not. Just being in his presence gave me all I needed to know.

Much of the retreat was in silence. Maintaining silence promoted the process of going inward. As Rinpoche explained, "Perfect peace comes through internal development of the mind. If you are not interacting with people, you will have more time to explore and develop your mind."

A bell rang, announcing the end of the lunch break. After we were all seated on our meditation cushions again, Rinpoche entered and we all rose. When he sat down, we each did three more prostrations before returning to our zafus (meditation cushions).

Then he posed a second question: "Why meditate?" He offered this rationale. "It makes the mind aware and helps to achieve right understanding. To become one with the object is the purpose of meditation."

What object? I asked myself. What is he talking about? I was getting lost again.

Before I could ask another question, Rinpoche turned to teaching us the body posture rules for meditating. The left leg should be up and the right leg should hang loose or cross-legged. The back should be straight with the head slightly tilted forward and the shoulders straight. The thumbs touching with the right hand lying in the left hand and both hands placed in the lap. The lips should be closed with the tongue touching the palate. The eyes were either closed or looking down.

Then Rinpoche focused on our breathing. "Concentrate on the breath coming from the right nostril in the form of light reaching all sentient beings and providing them with perfect peace. All suffering comes in the left nostril in the form of smoke representing the negative mind. It all goes to the heart, where it burns and becomes the sun, destroying all negativity."

Pretty heady stuff, I thought. But how could that actually work? How could my breathing out through my right nostril become light bringing peace to all sentient beings? I was skeptical. It couldn't be that easy.

After this brief training, we all got to practice meditating in silence for a couple of hours before a break for a light dinner. Then there was more discourse and meditation practice. It was close to 10:00 p.m. when we were dismissed and wandered down the hill to our primitive sleeping quarters. Very tired after a long day, I quickly fell asleep when I lay down on a straw mat and my head hit my makeshift pillow.

The next morning, we were awakened at 4:30 a.m. It was cold out and still pitch-black. Our early morning meditation session was to begin at five. The walk up the hill to the gompa would take ten to fifteen minutes, so we had to quickly get dressed, splash some water on our faces, and get going.

Every morning started this same way. In fact, every day for the first two weeks of the retreat followed the same rigorous schedule of eight hours of Rinpoche's discourses and six hours of meditation. The pattern was meditation followed by breakfast and discourse. Then more meditation, lunch, and more discourse. Then another round of meditation and discourse before dinner. The evening consisted of more discourse, more meditation, and finally, sleep.

I felt like we were in boot camp minus the overbearing sergeant, but it helped to have Lynda and Lenny there for support. We often ate meals together and shared our feelings about what we were experiencing. I told them I felt exhilarated learning about Tibetan Buddhism. At the same time, I was frustrated by my inability to sit still for a whole meditation session. By the evening, I was often exhausted and yearned for a good night's sleep.

What I found most fascinating were the images we were instructed to concentrate on as we meditated. One meditation focused on compassion. Visualizing all beings having been my mother for countless lifetimes greatly increased my caring for others, whether I knew them or not. I could see why Tibetans who embodied such a profound concept through their ongoing meditation were so loving.

Breakfast always provided a brief respite. It consisted of roasted barley porridge with a cup of butter tea, or *po cha*, which was comprised of black tea, yak butter, and salt. It took me a while to develop a taste for it, but eventually, I did.

During one morning discourse, Rinpoche emphasized the value of impulse in meditation. He explained that impulse was the most important aspect of meditation and dharma action. One's impulse, that is, motivation or strong desire, had to be pure for meditation to be powerful and effective. If one's meditation was not pure, then it could cause more suffering instead of the cessation of suffering.

"External developments [in the world] are not the principal cause of happiness. Too many external developments bring suffering. Thus, happiness and suffering both originate in the mind. Meditation is the method of escape from samsara [the endless wheel of life, death, and rebirth] and attainment of enlightenment."

It sounded so simple. But sitting still and meditating was far from it for me. First of all, I had difficulty finding a comfortable position I could hold. My left knee would begin to ache, so I moved slightly to alleviate my discomfort. Then I would have an itch on my right arm that I had to scratch after a while. Not much later my right foot started to bother me. After some time, I gave in and moved it to reduce the irritation. And on it went until the bell rang for lunch. I felt like a poor student failing Meditation 101. But I was not about to give up. If nothing else, I was persistent. After a while, I did settle down and stopped fidgeting around for the rest of the session. Yet, when the next meditation period began, I would experience the same rigamarole again.

Not only did I struggle with sitting still while meditating, I also had difficulty wrapping my head around some of the basic Buddhist concepts that Rinpoche presented. Still, I stuck with it while becoming the most vocal questioner in the hall. In truth, I was pretty skeptical of Tibetan Buddhism's very foundation. With little hesitation, I posed yet another question to Rinpoche. "How does ignorance produce greed and hatred?"

"Ignorance is the principal source of suffering," he replied. "It creates the illusion that problems are caused by external objects. But the dharma teaches that everything is a creation of the mind. The sufferings of sentient beings are created by their own minds. So also, enlightenment is created by one's own mind. If perfect peace depended on material possessions, we would have clearly achieved it. But perfect peace must be achieved through the mind, changing the mind from negative to positive. Wealth doesn't stop suffering or eliminate the negative mind."

No, I said to myself, but being wealthy could help people overcome at least some of their suffering. At the same time, I thought about all the poor Indian people I had observed over the last four months. While I couldn't get into their heads, I had the impression that, for the most part, they had accepted their impoverished state, as well as their low position in society. I sensed that unlike most Westerners, the desire or craving for something more was not a major cause of their suffering. Like billions of impoverished people around the globe, they suffered because they were hungry or lacked adequate shelter. It was a matter of survival, not unfulfilled hopes and desires. Ironically, my craving for greater understanding became the source of my own suffering. As always, my hungry ghost wanted more.

Rinpoche began one morning's discourse by exploring the nature of karma, the law of cause and effect. He said that understanding karma was the best solution to the suffering mind. Again, I was puzzled and quickly raised my hand. "Rinpoche, what do you mean?"

"One's karma all depends on the state of mind with which the action is performed," he explained. "Karmic action depends on motive. Good karma comes from good motives, while bad karma is the result of selfish or greedy motives. Karma is carried with the mind from one lifetime to the next."

Now I was really lost. What was he talking about? Did my good karma from a prior life bring me to this Buddhist retreat? How could what happened in a prior life—if there even was such a thing—possibly affect what I did in this life? My desire for greater understanding was only causing me more frustration, more suffering. Was I trapped in the cycle of death and rebirth?

"The ignorant mind is concerned with stopping temporal suffering," Rinpoche said. "True happiness is only derived through the renunciation of all desires. This true happiness can never end, unlike ordinary happiness, which is fleeting."

Still puzzled, I was beginning to get a glimpse of what Rinpoche was getting at. My attachment to temporal desires, my ignorant mind, was the source of my unhappiness, my suffering. I was attached to my body, my possessions, my position in life, and my relationships. My happiness depended on whether I perceived these things as positive or negative. All my attachments arose from my needs and wants. By practicing the dharma and nonattachment, I could free myself of that dependence and achieve true happiness according to Tibetan Buddhism.

Maybe, I thought, but obtaining true nonattachment was a huge mountain to climb.

Rinpoche advised that the key to achieving real happiness was meditating regularly. He emphasized that the purpose of meditation was to clean the ignorant or negative mind. The negative mind was like a mirror covered with *kaka*, or dung. When the mirror was cleaned, the intrinsic nature of the mind, the pure mind, was visible and one could achieve true happiness or enlightenment.

Rinpoche continued that what got in our way was our concept of the independent, self-existing "I." But through meditation, we could rid ourselves of that idea. As long as we saw ourselves as separate, independent individuals, we would continue to be attached to our temporal possessions and relationships. And that would keep us in a state of desire and suffering. So we needed to let go of our self-existent egos through meditation.

That was a lot to take in. Letting go of my independent self was a very tall order.

On the tenth morning of the retreat, Rinpoche addressed meditations to renounce our attachments. He noted that meditating on the impermanence of life, as well as on the indefiniteness of the time of death, was extremely helpful. Focusing on these ideas made one more concerned with future lives and suffering rather than one's present life and problems, he explained. As a result, one's meditation was less distracted by temporal needs.

He gave the following example. "Someone says something that makes me angry. I meditate on getting angry and realize that it's silly to get angry because life is so indefinite. My life may not continue for another hour. Getting angry now in the short-term will create bad karma, causing greater suffering in my future life.

"Meditation is very useful for all situations that cause temporal discomfort, uneasiness, pain, jealousy, and other negative emotions. It keeps one at peace, calm, and in control of all situations. While I'm attached to these feelings, my mind will never be peaceful. Meditation makes one relaxed and in control. Attachment just makes one uptight."

That really struck a chord with me. Holding on to my negative feelings only made me more miserable. But what I didn't get was the idea that my karma traveled with me from one lifetime to the next. How could I have multiple lifetimes? When I died, I was dead. Wasn't that true? I wanted to understand reincarnation from a Buddhist perspective, but he stayed focused on the mind and the creation of karma.

"Suffering and happiness are creations of one's own mind. Mind doesn't fully realize the nature of suffering. We need to practice the dharma to realize it. Craving is the principal cause of the hell states. Miserliness is the principal cause of the hungry spirit. As we see suffering more clearly, we become more careful in the creation of our karma."

Then Rinpoche took the importance of realizing the nature of suffering to a higher level. "Realizing the true nature of our suffering leads to achieving great compassion for all sentient beings. When we experience our unbearable suffering, we understand other beings' suffering is unbearable, and we have great compassion. But we enjoy creating the cause of our suffering, that is, earthly pleasures, so we continue to experience samsara. Meditating on our suffering helps release us from samsara and future suffering."

At that point, Rinpoche said we were ready to take refuge after having received almost two weeks of the Buddha's teachings. The purpose of taking refuge was to release us from samsara, the endless cycle of suffering life, death, and rebirth. By taking refuge, we retreatants would be proclaiming our aspiration to lead a life with the three jewels—the Buddha, the dharma, and the sangha (the Buddhist community)—at its core. It was our expression of determination to follow the Buddha's path.

"Buddha is the doctor who prescribes the medicine," Rinpoche noted. "Dharma is the medicine that cures the mental suffering. And the Sangha are the nurses, the community, who help the patient recover from the illness of samsaric suffering."

He cautioned that we needed to have two prerequisites before taking refuge. First, great fear of suffering from samsara. And second, we needed a firm belief that the three jewels had the sublime power to guide us to freedom from suffering.

Together, we all repeated after Rinpoche, "I take refuge in the Buddha. I take refuge in the Dharma. I take refuge in the Sangha."

Rinpoche reminded us that taking refuge was the path to releasing our suffering and attaining enlightenment. He defined enlightenment as the realization of the intrinsic nature of our minds: an omniscient state of mind having the ability to perceive everything, including the beginningless mind. In other words, there was no beginning or end of mind from one lifetime to the next. And there was no way to go back any further than that.

"The mind is beginningless," he said. "It is only due to the continuity of the mind that we can develop the mind to the point of enlightenment."

It was this last point that I found really perplexing. Mind continues from one lifetime to the next with no beginning or end. How could that be?

On top of that, Rinpoche emphasized that our suffering continued because we failed to understand the duality of our temporal mind, which saw things as either negative or positive. He asserted that we could not escape from samsara if we didn't recognize this duality, which was at the core of our suffering.

I slowly began to see that it was our ego, the self-existing "I," that continued to get in the way, always judging whether something was good or bad, ugly or pretty, ignorant or intelligent, and so on. By practicing dharma, we could reject the negative mind's illusive perceptions and develop the positive mind.

"The essence of the dharma is creating good karma and avoiding bad karma," he stressed. "The principal cause of happiness is internal, the state of our mind. Practicing the dharma helps to free the mind of greed, hatred, and ignorance and creates good karma. It is for the benefit of all sentient beings. If we observe an object or person with compassion and think positively, we can work for the happiness and peace of all sentient beings. This way, we reject the negative mind and create good rather than bad karma."

I still wasn't sold on Buddhism as the miracle formula that would eliminate my suffering and lead me to true happiness. But I felt that as long as I was in this month-long retreat, I should stick to the program. There was still a little more than two weeks to go. Who knew what would happen next?

15

GETTING ON THE PATH TO ENLIGHTENMENT

On day fifteen of the Buddhist meditation retreat, we all took precepts in a ritual conducted by Rinpoche at 5:00 a.m. Buddhist precepts are vows meant to develop one's mind and character to make progress on the path to enlightenment. Some of them are similar to the Ten Commandments. Others are even more restrictive.

We pledged to abide by these eight precepts: no killing; no stealing; no sexual intercourse or release; no lying; no taking intoxicants; no sleeping on a soft, comfortable bed; no eating after noon and only once in the morning; and no wearing perfume or jewelry and no dancing or singing.

Rinpoche explained that failing to observe any one of these precepts would hinder movement toward enlightenment.

Fortunately, we vowed to honor the precepts just for the duration of the retreat, which was only two more weeks. It was sort of a dry run for us to get a taste of living a Tibetan Buddhist life.

Before our morning meditation the next day, we vowed to abide by the eight precepts again. This would be our practice every day for the rest of the retreat. Then Rinpoche focused on karma. His description gave me a very different perspective on how we are all interconnected, one I had never considered before.

"All karma is related. Just as there is no self-existing "I," so there cannot be any self-existing karma. My karma affects many others, just as their karma affects me. Each karmic action sets off a chain reaction that is endless and which has a multiplying effect. In reality, the world consists of one large chain of karmic action, all interdependent. This is true for both bad and good karma. So the purer I can develop my mind, the more good karma I can create and the more good karma will be created from that.

"Also, I cannot divorce myself from others' karma. The vibration from others' karma will eventually affect me. It is my responsibility, in order to reach enlightenment for the sake of all sentient beings, to create good karma and encourage others to do the same.

"We are all one. If we are to have peace in the world, we must work out our karma together."

I could hardly believe it. Rinpoche, this young, humble, reincarnated (if I embraced Buddhist teachings) monk was conveying a universal message. This concept that we were all one seemed to be coming from his intrinsic mind, the essential nature of all humanity, which he had experienced in endless prior lives. It seemed to me that Rinpoche had reincarnated in his current lifetime to pass on this ancient wisdom, the dharma, to the West.

At the same time, a dazzling burst of light went off in my head. The tragic karma the Tibetans suffered due to the 1959 Chinese invasion of Tibet created the impetus for the positive karma we were now benefiting from. If the Chinese incursion had not forced Rinpoche and his fellow Tibetans to flee their homeland, then he and other lamas would not be disseminating the dharma to thousands of people all over the world.

I was getting what Buddhism was all about on a cellular level. Yes, we really were all one! I was feeling a transformational energy on both an intense spiritual and deeply soulful level. But I had no words for it. Suddenly, my understanding of the world took a 180-degree turn. From being the most vocal skeptic in the retreat, I instantly became a true believer.

This ancient credo was exactly what Ram Dass, the Beatles, the musical, *Hair*, and other New Age voices were proclaiming to millions of Westerners about the Age of Aquarius. I'd gone halfway around the world to receive this ageless insight from its very source.

Rinpoche then proceeded to go into an extensive explanation of karma. Most importantly, he said, "Understanding of the law of karma is essential to the practice of the dharma and can bring enlightenment." He explained that without an understanding of karmic law, one could not control the mind and find peace and happiness.

As I lay down that night, I began to get a clearer picture of the interconnection between the mind, the ego, and karma. According to the dharma, everything, including the ego and karma, originates in the mind. The intrinsic mind, the energy field that encompasses the entire universe, is both beginningless and endless, just like the sky above. Our temporal mind creates the illusion that our ego is self-existing and that we are independent of one another. It generates thoughts that create karma that creates more karma and on and on. But the intrinsic mind is the same for all sentient beings: one interconnected domain. Since our karma is interconnected by this field of energy, we are all affected by it.

I began to grasp the importance of deep meditation as the vehicle for letting go of our attachments to our temporal possessions and relationships created by our egos. That sounded really good but extremely difficult to achieve, regardless of how many lifetimes I might try. In addition, I wondered how the mind existed from one lifetime to the next.

In my temporal mind, it all came down to believing in reincarnation, something that had yet to be mentioned by name even though we were already in the third week of the retreat. But maybe there was another way of looking at it. If there were a timeless, universal mind, then we all must be part of it.

In fact, I experienced this phenomenon myself during the retreat with Dorothy, a total stranger from Wyoming. She sat on the other side of the gompa from me. At times during the retreat, we nonverbally communicated with each other from a distance. It felt like some kind of telepathy to me.

During our lunch break one day, Dorothy and I discussed what we had been going through during the retreat. Somehow, we knew when each other was really moved by something Rinpoche was saying and even when one of us was hungry. From across the room, we shared a vibration or extrasensory connection. Were we tuning in to the intrinsic mind we all shared?

I was seeing everything through a different lens now. The intrinsic mind had taken over. My ego was no longer in control.

I was letting go of my independent "I." In that moment, I had no ego, no separateness. Just oneness with everything. But it didn't last. In a matter of seconds, I was pulled back into the meditation retreat ambiance. At that moment, I heard Rinpoche explain, "Just as [a] flower grows from seed, so the enlightened mind comes from the intrinsic nature of our minds." I could feel that seed opening inside me and the emerging bud beginning to reach for the enlightened mind. My positive karma was bearing fruit. I started to see how everything in my life was connected and how all I had experienced up until that moment had driven me here.

For instance, my parents had given me three thousand dollars as a present when I graduated from law school in 1970. Adding some of my own money to that, I bought a little sports car. If I had not graduated law school, I would not have gotten their generous gift or been able to afford my car. In 1972, I sold that car to get the money to take my trip. If I had not met with my former girlfriend and her husband after their return from India, I would not have traveled to India and Nepal. If I had not run into my acquaintances from law school in Kathmandu, I would not have known about the retreat. If my cousin Eddie hadn't canceled his wedding, I would not have changed my flight, which allowed me to stay in Nepal and attend the Kopan retreat. In one way or another, everything was connected. Suddenly, it was all making sense.

During the next week, Rinpoche addressed the suffering of samsara, the beginningless and endless cycle of birth, life, death, and rebirth. He noted the eight causes of suffering according to Buddhism: rebirth, old age, sickness, death, attachment to beautiful objects, encounters with ugly or disagreeable objects, not obtaining desirable objects, and the suffering of the body created by delusion and karma.

As he spoke, I thought about how my life was filled with the suffering of samsara. I'd been attached to getting into the best college and law school. I'd searched endlessly for a long-term relationship with a desirable woman. My mind was trapped in samsara.

Following the discussion on samsara and its causes, Rinpoche introduced a meditation on sunyata, emptiness, to assist us in our escape from this suffering. The meditation focused on the emptiness of all phenomena: objects, subjects, and relationships. All phenomena were interdependent, impermanent, and relative. All lacked intrinsic nature or self-essence.

We spent the rest of the morning meditating on sunyata, deepening our sense of our own emptiness. As I became more immersed in the meditation, I began to recognize how my attachment to things, relationships, and all phenomena hindered my path to oneness.

After lunch, we learned that observing karma was the best way to cross the ocean of suffering successfully. Rinpoche explained that we must have faith in the law of karma and the fear of death to proceed on the path. "This fear keeps one away from attachment, greed, ignorance, and hatred. Fear of death creates much energy with which to practice dharma, keep precepts, and prevent laziness. One needs to generate mental discipline to not be attached in body, speech, or mind."

While I had never paid much attention to the fear of death, I could see how it could motivate me, just like the fear of becoming very ill or losing my lover. Practicing the dharma would not prevent those things from happening. Rather, my practice would lessen my attachment to those things and in turn reduce my fear.

After an evening break, Rinpoche shifted to a meditation on restlessness. I thought he must have intuitively known that many of us were feeling restless. Or maybe he just saw that many of us, including me, were having difficulty sitting still. This meditation was something I certainly needed. "To rejoice in the fullness of this moment is all the peace I can ever hope for," he said. "There is no other moment."

Like the other meditations we were learning, it didn't provide instant relief or nirvana. Meditation was a practice. Day after day, I wrestled with my restless mind. Some days I failed to quiet it. Other days I found some peace of mind. Regardless, the meditation helped me go deeper into examining how my mind functioned. Mental control was key to my developing a solid meditation practice.

On the morning of day twenty, we were given another new meditation: "Everything is in accordance with natural law. The rain falls, the wind blows, and the tree grows. Man alone, deluded by superiority, attempts to change the rules. Desiring a more favored position in the garden, he suffers endlessly for his sin."

So simple, I thought, yet not really. My life was filled with distractions, desires, and delusions. While learning this new way of thinking and being, I still wanted a loving relationship, a nice car, a comfortable home, and a good job. I was still attached to many phenomena and not ready to let go. I clung to the belief that these things would make me happy.

But Rinpoche had an answer to my longings. "If one enjoys pleasures without greed and with a fully renounced mind, one will not suffer in samsara. By following greed, suffering will occur in the future, though the immediate result may be samsaric pleasure.

"Samsara is a trap baited by fleeting happiness but causing lasting suffering. All samsaric happiness is in the nature of suffering. Material possessions are not the cause of suffering. Negative mind is. So renunciation doesn't depend on giving up all possessions."

That was good news, but I wondered how I could renounce my negative mind? Since childhood, I was aware that my negative mind had been influencing my behavior, so much so that I was voted class pessimist in ninth grade. I reflected on how my mother's judgmental attitude had triggered my frequent feelings that neither I nor the things in my life were good enough. I was excited to have an opportunity to rid myself of that.

On day twenty-one of the retreat, Rinpoche introduced the Mahayana method, the form of Buddhism practiced by Tibetans. To renounce the negative mind, Mahayana taught that one must aspire to bodhicitta, a mind aimed at awakening with great love and compassion for the benefit of all sentient beings. To attain bodhicitta, one had to practice the six paramitas or guides to enlightenment: charity, morality, patience, effort, concentration, and wisdom. This required embracing the Four Noble Truths.

The first Noble Truth is the truth of suffering, often stated as life is suffering. Rinpoche noted that suffering is impermanent or temporary, continuously changing, and not independent. It is a state of mind in which we are never fully satisfied. I knew that my hungry ghost had a role in all this.

The second Noble Truth is the truth of the cause of suffering. Our actions (karma) and delusions are the principal causes of suffering. We bring about our suffering through our inability to see or accept the true reality of ourselves or the world around us. Our attitudes and actions are the primary determining factors of our happiness or suffering.

The third Noble Truth is the truth of the end of suffering. One can be permanently free from the ignorance and attachment that cause suffering.

The fourth Noble Truth is the truth of the path to the cessation of suffering. It is the path to full renunciation of samsara and the realization of non-selfness.

The four Noble Truths pulled it all together for me. They gave me a whole new way of seeing my world. I no longer had to be the victim of whatever the world threw at me. Instead, I could be in control. If I could train my mind to be detached from karma—accepting what is without judgment—I could free myself from suffering and achieve real peace of mind. I just needed to develop a strong, persistent meditation practice, which I knew would not be easy.

More time was devoted to meditation and less to Rinpoche's discourses during the last week of the retreat. He continued to emphasize that meditation practice was the key to escaping from samsara and realizing true lasting happiness.

As the retreat ended, I felt I had been reborn. I had a whole new way of relating to myself and all phenomena. I was lighter, a bit emptier, and eager to put what I had learned to the test of living my life according to the Four Noble Truths.

16

REENTERING THE TEMPORAL WORLD

IN CELEBRATION OF OUR COMPLETING the retreat, many lamas and monks of all ages arrived to conduct a ritual ceremony called a puja that honored the memory of the Buddha. Curious, smiling boys, some no more than six or seven, along with their monastic elders, eagerly posed in their full-length maroon robes as I captured them with my Minolta 35 mm camera. Perhaps forty or more came from considerable distances to join in the festivities. I was humbled and very pleased by their presence.

After such an intensive month of learning and meditation, I felt both full and empty at the same time: full of Tibetan Buddhist teachings and visualizations I had received during the retreat and emptied of my ego-driven mind. Perhaps I was not totally emptied of my ego-driven mind, but surely a wide-open space had replaced the normal chatter that regularly cluttered my brain. I let go of worrying about my parents' reactions, how I looked, and what I would do when I got back to the States—at least for the time being.

By mid-afternoon, I expressed my deep gratitude and bid sad farewells to Lama Yeshe and Thupten Zopa Rinpoche, hugged the friends I had made during the retreat, and acknowledged how much I would miss them all. As I started the trek back to Kathmandu, I had yet to recognize the extent of the alterations my body and mind had undergone during my time at Kopan. While I had shed more than a few pounds, my consciousness had experienced a much greater transformation. Not until I arrived back in the city did I begin to grasp how much I had changed and the nature of my new self.

As I walked through the streets of the capital, I felt like a visitor from another planet. Nothing seemed real. I could have been Dorothy wandering through Oz. Or Alice, having just landed in Wonderland. The plants, buildings, people in the streets—everything—had a bright, otherworldly, magical glow. I had never experienced anything like it before, not even while tripping on acid.

Slowly, however, I lost my lightness of being. After a couple of days, that glimmering shine disappeared. Still, I wasn't quite back to my pre-retreat "normal." I had a heightened sense of awareness. My perspective had deepened in a way I could not quite describe, but I could feel it in my heart and bones.

Much to my delight, I had the opportunity to participate in a very different spiritual experience the next evening. I attended a Passover seder hosted by the Israeli Ambassador to Nepal. Fellow travelers, as well as local Jews and embassy employees, perhaps a total of forty guests, gathered at the ambassador's home to celebrate the Jewish people's exodus from Egypt more than twenty-five hundred years ago. In a warm and friendly atmosphere, we ate, prayed, and sang well into the night. It brought back fond memories of many past seders with friends and family in the States, making me feel a bit homesick. Having been immersed in Eastern culture and carefree living, I hadn't had such nostalgic feelings in months.

Passover had always been my favorite Jewish holiday. In essence, the seder celebrated the universal desire for freedom, both physically and spiritually. That night at the ambassador's home we sang "Go Down Moses."

> When Israel was in Egypt land,
> Let my people go!
> Oppressed so hard they could not stand,
> Let my people go!
>
> Go down, Moses,
> Way down in Egypt land,
> Tell ol' Pharoah,
> Let my people go.

In a broader interpretation of the hymn, the pharaoh and Egypt represented more than the physical bondage of the Jewish people. The hymn was calling for spiritual and emotional freedom as well. And not just for Jews but for all people. Having recently completed the Kopan retreat, I felt a similar release from my limited egocentric, temporal mind as I sang "Let my people go."

Jumping from one ancient tradition to another reaffirmed Rinpoche's primary lesson. While the religious ceremonies and practices of the Buddhists and Jews were distinctly different, I experienced a spiritual simpatico between the two. I realized that they professed the same message: We are all one. Each of us is a piece of the single cosmic fabric, the intrinsic mind, that makes up our world, calling for universal freedom.

The following morning, I wrote my folks about the very spirited seder at the ambassador's home the previous night. I knew they would be pleased that I had not lost touch with my Jewish roots so far away from home. While reassuring them of my continued connection to Judaism despite having just completed a Buddhist retreat, I also could not withhold sharing my very moving experience at the Kopan monastery with them. "It just might have been the most important month of my life, a real turning point. But you can judge for yourselves soon enough. (Don't worry, I'm not converting.)"

Given my parents' serious apprehensions about my extended journey, I had second thoughts about expressing how deeply moved I was by the retreat. Still, I wanted to be honest and tried to prepare them for the new me who would soon be arriving back home.

A few days later, I was gazing through the window of a vintage, ten-seater Cessna aircraft at the snowy Himalayan mountaintops while flying to the small town of Pokhara (population twenty-four thousand) in western Nepal. The gateway to the Annapurna Range, the town was just thirty-five miles from three of the ten highest peaks in the world. The short flight gave me a breathtaking view of those majestic mountains. One day I was getting high on Tibetan Buddhism and a few days later I was soaring over those mighty peaks. I began wondering if there might be some connection between the mountains and Buddhism.

The more I thought about it, the more I realized there had to be a correlation. The sacred Inca civilization developed high in the Andes Mountains of South America. The Aztecs lived in the mountains of Mexico. And the ancient Greeks worshiped the majestic Mount Olympus, where they believed the thrones of Zeus and his divine family resided. Could it be that, like the Tibetan Buddhists, these other societies lived near or in the mountains because they thought it brought them closer to their gods or the Great Spirit? The air is thinner in higher elevations. Perhaps these cultures felt lighter in those elevated regions with their thinner air and believed that made it easier to communicate with the gods. Being in the Himalayas, I definitely experienced a lightness of being that lifted my spirit.

I was running out of time before I had to be back in Delhi to catch my flight to Amsterdam on May 13. That date was set in stone since my roundtrip ticket back to New York would expire in mid-May. But I wanted to at least get a closer glimpse of the Himalayas while I still had the chance. My hungry ghost would not let go of its desire to view those awesome peaks.

Originally, I had planned to do a two-week trek on the Annapurna circuit, but opting to take the Mahayana training eliminated that possibility. There just weren't enough days left. Short on time and without proper gear, I had to settle for a couple of day hikes outside of Pokhara. Though disappointed in not being able to do an extended trek, I couldn't help falling in love with the grandeur of the Annapurna range.

The massif was thirty-four miles long and contained Annapurna 1. At 26,545 feet, it was the tenth-highest mountain in the world. Nearby, Dhaulagiri 1 was the seventh-highest at 26,795 feet. Rising from lush, green meadows and forests, these giants of nature covered with tons of snow were beyond amazing.

My day hikes through the Annapurna foothills were unforgettable. The terraced fields and traditional Gurung villages with the majestic mountains rising behind them filled me with unspeakable joy. Surrounded by such beauty, I was elated and promised myself that I would be back someday to trek the circuit and have a more intimate experience with their magic.

Way too soon, I boarded the bus to Sonauli, the Indian border town where I would catch a train back to New Delhi. The bus ride from Pokhara through the mountains was over six hundred miles. Usually, it took close to sixteen hours, but my ride was anything but normal.

Several hours into the trip, we were suddenly stopped dead in our tracks by an avalanche. Fifty or more buses and trucks were backed up on each side of a huge mound of snow and ice blocking the narrow mountain road. After learning what was happening, I got out of the bus to stretch my legs and get a closer look at the extent of the roadblock. As I walked toward the massive avalanche, I met a fellow American traveler dressed all in white. His name was John, and he was a few years younger than me.

We exchanged a little information about ourselves and our journeys. A bit wearily, John told me that he had been on the road for months. But his voice lifted when he explained, "I'm on a pilgrimage to Lumbini, the birthplace of the Buddha. It's about fifteen miles from Sonauli on the Nepalese side of the border. It's been a long trip, but I'm finally getting there."

I began imagining going there myself. "The place where the Buddha was born? Really?"

I had already been to Bodh Gaya, where the Buddha was enlightened, and Sarnath where he gave his first sermon, two of the four holiest sites in Buddhism. But I had no idea I was now so close to a third holy place. If it were not for this spontaneous force of nature, I would not have met John nor learned about Lumbini.

It was a timely miracle, I thought. Like all the seeming coincidences that led me to the Kopan retreat, I sensed some kind of divine intervention was leading me to the Buddha's birthplace. I didn't believe in accidents. In my way of thinking, everything happened for a reason, though we might have no idea what that reason was. The universe was either a frenetic blob of chaotic energy without any rhyme or reason or an interconnected web of intelligent energy. I believed the latter was true, in accordance with what I had just learned about the Buddhist concept of the intrinsic mind and Rinpoche's teaching that we are all one.

Many hours later, a crew of Nepalese men finished shoveling the massive pile of snow and ice off the road, and we were on our way again. The next morning, we finally reached Sonauli. Tired from the extremely long ride, I stumbled off the bus, threw my pack on my back, and began walking to the train station.

Suddenly, my inner voice called to me: *Go to Lumbini. You'll never be back here again. The birthplace of the Buddha is a very special place.*

How could I not go? So after gathering my toothbrush, toothpaste, water bottle, and sleeping bag, I secured my backpack in a locker at the train station. With the aid of a station attendant, I found my way to the road to Lumbini and began walking.

Nearing the end of April, the temperature was around ninety-five degrees. It hadn't rained in that part of the world since the previous September. The dusty road was hot and dry with no shade, and I had fifteen long miles ahead of me. But off I went, determined to get to the Buddha's birthplace.

There were no cars or trucks on the road, and no one else walking. Once in a while I came to a lone tree, took a short break, and drank a little water as drops of sweat rolled down my face.

After a couple of hours, what looked like a US Army surplus Jeep appeared out of nowhere and stopped alongside me. There in the front passenger's seat sat John, the guy I'd met the day before while waiting for the avalanche to be cleared. I was stunned and overjoyed.

"Hi! Hop in," John said, greeting me. I gladly did as his Nepalese driver made room for me in the rear of the Jeep. "I hitched a ride on the edge of town with this nice fellow who was going to Lumbini," he said. What had taken me over two hours to walk, John had traveled in ten minutes by Jeep. Relieved that my trek in the scorching heat was over, I couldn't have been more grateful for the ride.

When we arrived in Lumbini, our driver dropped us off at the government guesthouse. Since tourist season had not yet begun, John and I were the only ones in the entire place. It was a cinderblock building with minimal décor. We each had a room with a simple cot, a chair, and a small chest of drawers. Most importantly, it kept us sheltered from the sizzling sun.

In addition to the guesthouse, there was a small Buddhist temple nearby where pilgrims came to pay homage to the Buddha. Lumbini was out in the middle of nowhere and could hardly be called a town. It had only one narrow dirt road lined on both sides with open-air shops where tourists could buy all kinds of souvenirs or get some simple Indian food. Since

I didn't see anything that looked like houses, I imagined the shopkeepers lived in the rear of their humble booths.

I was exhausted after a long, hot day, so I grabbed a basic Indian meal of chapatis and dal for dinner and then went back to my room in the guesthouse and quickly fell asleep. I was way too tired to even think about my birthday the next day when I would turn twenty-eight.

17

MAKING AN INTIMATE CONNECTION WITH THE BUDDHA

It felt like some supernatural force had arranged a mystical birthday experience for me. I was at the birthplace of the Buddha on my twenty-eighth birthday. Both the Buddha and I were born under the April full moon, only twenty-five hundred years apart. It seemed very auspicious being in this sacred place on my birthday.

Of course, it wouldn't have happened but for so many prior events falling into place without my lifting a finger. A series of synchronistic events brought about my attending the retreat at Kopan, which had resulted in my deep dive into Tibetan Buddhism and discovering a new way of being.

As all these incidents were occurring, I had no idea where they were leading me. Nor did my hungry ghost understand they were guiding me to where its cravings would be satisfied and my journey would achieve the meaning I had been seeking for so long. The success of my extended odyssey exponentially boosted my belief that you don't have to know where you're going to get where you want to be.

Buddha was said to have begun his spiritual quest when he was twenty-nine. It seemed those same mystical forces were putting me on that path a year earlier. Could I have been ready to pursue the way to enlightenment sooner than the Buddha? I seriously doubted that. Maybe I had to start a bit earlier in my life because it was going to take me longer to get there. It really didn't matter. I just felt very fortunate to have gotten on the path.

But there was another intriguing aspect of my being in Lumbini as I was turning twenty-eight. According to astrology, between twenty-seven and about thirty, people experienced their first Saturn Return. That is, the planet Saturn was now occupying the same place in the heavens it had when I was born. Remarkably, the Buddha and I both began our spiritual quests during our Saturn Returns.

Astrologers believed that one's Saturn Return signaled a time for a major course correction in one's life. It was said to be when one found greater structure and laid a stronger foundation for the future. Each Saturn Return ushered in another stage of life. Whatever new direction was revealed around this time would continue to develop throughout one's life.

My journey undoubtedly launched a significant course correction in my life. I found a whole new worldview due to Tibetan Buddhism. I now saw myself as intricately part of a universal energy rather than as an independent individual acting alone. I just had no idea how that would affect me or how it would play out once I returned to the States.

My twenty-eighth birthday was one of the most amazing days of my life. I began by sitting under the Bodhi tree (actually a descendant of the original Bodhi tree) where Queen Maya Devi gave birth to Siddhartha Gautama, who was to become the Enlightened One. I imagined that maybe I had some providential tie to the Buddha and the dharma.

I soon dropped into a deep state of meditation. My mind began letting go of all thoughts and musings. I could feel a soft energy permeating every cell of my being. My body, mind, and spirit were settling into a quiet peace. As I fell into a vast emptiness, I heard a voice calling out to me from deep within my being, *Buddha is my brother*. Strangely, the first letter of "Buddha," "my," and "brother" corresponded to my initials, BMB. My soul seemed to be telling me that I was related to the Buddha. He was my brother. I was spellbound.

Perhaps I was being beckoned to a timeless, open space. A place that was always there but had been obscured by my busy lifestyle and my hungry ghost continuously striving to achieve something. I had no idea where all this was coming from or where it might be taking me. I was an empty vessel and had no control over any of it. The being that I had always known had disappeared. There was no me, just nothingness.

When I left Kopan, I'd thought the Buddhist seed planted in me would take time to sprout. But now that seed was, indeed, beginning to sprout. My newly acquired understanding of the dharma, though limited, gave me a very different outlook on life. On a molecular level, I was experiencing that everything was interconnected. I was a small piece of one huge pie, the all-encompassing universe. Awestruck, in some remarkable way, I felt I was being reborn. I had no words to describe it, though I felt it in every cell of my body.

I had totally lost track of time while in this meditative state. But sometime later, I stood up under the Bodhi tree. I felt lighter, almost floating, like some heavy weight had been lifted off me. I turned and observed a small, modest Buddhist temple just a few steps away. With the hot afternoon sun beating down on me, I decided to check out the temple to avoid being overcome by the unbearable heat.

As I entered the simple shrine, I noticed that my fellow traveler, John, was the only other person there. No monks or other visitors were there. We acknowledged each other's presence without words.

A huge, golden Buddha opposite the entrance caught my attention and instantly drew me toward it. The statue must have been at least twenty feet tall. I imagined it had been constructed inside the temple since there was no way it could have made it through the entrance in one piece.

I sat in silence gazing at this all-encompassing figure until I began nodding off. I hadn't eaten anything all day and was beginning to feel weak. At that point, I decided the only thing to do was go back to the guest house and rest.

I left the sanctuary and was immediately overpowered by a raging sandstorm. Putting my left forearm over my eyes to block the sand, I could barely see five feet in front of me. I fought my way through the fierce winds, slowly advancing toward what I believed to be the direction of the guest house. By the time I reached my room, I was covered in sand and utterly exhausted. After brushing off the sand as best I could, I lay down and soon fell fast asleep.

When I awoke two hours later, the wind had died down. Looking through the window, I could see a steady rain falling outside. It was the first rainfall on the entire Indian subcontinent since the previous September. I smiled from ear to ear. Another sign of rebirth, I thought, as I pinched myself to be sure I wasn't dreaming. It was a birthday to top all birthdays and one I knew I would never forget.

There are just a few moments in most of our lives that we can consider truly transformative. That day in Lumbini was the culmination of my entire trip, as well as my life up to that point.

18

MAKING MY WAY BACK HOME

I WAS BOTH EXCITED AND anxious as I settled into my seat on the KLM Royal Dutch Airlines jet that would take me from New Delhi to Amsterdam. While I was thrilled to be on my way home after being away for so long, I was a bit uneasy about being squeezed into an economy seat with limited legroom for almost ten hours.

I was a lot more anxious, however, about my forthcoming reunion with my parents. While I was looking forward to seeing them, I worried about how they would react to my scruffy, full-grown beard and my long, straggly hair, a striking makeover from the well-groomed son they wished safe travels to a year earlier.

I knew it would not be easy for them. But how much a barrier my hippie appearance would be to our reconnecting, I could only guess. Until then I really hadn't given that much thought. Prior to my trip, I had considered my parents pretty open-minded. Now I wasn't so sure. When their own son looked like I did, they might not be so accepting.

As the plane took off, I tried to get those thoughts out of my mind. I pondered how I would respond to the way they greeted me and how I would react when my mother, who was not one to withhold her thoughts or feelings, started criticizing the way I looked. I began thinking our reunion could go south pretty quickly. A quiet anxiety started overtaking my entire being.

Fortunately, the flight attendant interrupted the mind game I was playing in my head. "Something to drink?" she asked.

"Ah, coffee, please, cream, no sugar." I thanked her as she poured a cup and handed it to me.

While I drank my coffee, I realized I needed something to take my mind off my upcoming reunion with my parents. I began drifting back to Kopan and hearing Rinpoche say that everything is a creation of the mind. "Eliminate the negative mind," Rinpoche had counseled us. Easier said than done, I thought.

But he had also explained that the key to getting rid of the negative mind was meditation. So I closed my eyes and tried meditating in my seat on the plane. After a while, my mind settled down some. I realized how attached I was to my parents' approval and how I always had been. My happiness seemed, to a large extent, dependent on what they thought about me and what I did. If I wanted to be truly happy, I had to let go of my attachment to their approval. My year of traveling abroad had certainly helped loosen my need for their blessing, but I still had a ways to go.

On a deeper level, I needed to detach myself from my ego—my identification as an independent, self-existing "I." It was my ego that craved my parents' approval, not my intrinsic being. Intellectually, I knew the truth of this, but I was far from incorporating it into my life and the core of my being. That would take a great deal of practice. Perhaps years of it. I decided I had better meditate more, a lot more, if I were to even come close to letting go of my ego and being my authentic self.

As I tried to meditate, my mind began to drift. I started envisioning a return to India. I saw myself working in the States to save enough money to travel back to the East by the following spring. At the same time, I would lay the foundation for an import business on the east coast that would sell Indian wares—soapstone pipes and Buddhas along with Indian sarongs and shirts—to the younger generation that had recently been turned on to Eastern spirituality by Ram Dass and the Beatles. While building my business, I would study Buddhism and deepen my meditation practice. I had it all worked out.

There was just one problem: my parents again. They would never go for my idea. No amount of explaining or visioning would ever convince them. My attachment to their approval smacked me right across the face. As long as I felt the need or desire for my parents' blessing, my dream would remain just a dream. I began to realize that I, and not my parents, was the real problem. Once again, I decided I'd better meditate more, a lot more.

Having fallen asleep while meditating, I awoke as a flight attendant walked down the aisle making sure passengers had their seat belts fastened. Over the loudspeaker, the copilot was informing us that we were beginning our descent into the Amsterdam airport. My pulse quickened as I became excited about returning to Amsterdam and being that much closer to home.

Amsterdam was one of my favorite places in Europe. I recalled my visit from the previous summer: the Heineken brewery tour, the Anne Frank hideaway, the Van Gogh Museum, the canals, and all the beautiful flowers everywhere. I loved Amsterdam. But I was on a mission to get back home and had no time to revisit any of that.

The next day I was on a plane to Philadelphia.

While I was able to get some sleep as we flew across the ocean, by the time we landed in Philly, my anxiety had reared its ugly head again. Deplaning and walking to retrieve my backpack from the luggage carousel, I continually heard Rinpoche softly telling me to let go of my negative thoughts and quiet my mind. By the time I picked up my pack and hurried through the terminal to meet my parents, I had calmed down considerably. I was as ready as I could be, all things considered, for my reunion with Mom and Dad.

Tears rolled down my face as I approached my folks. They greeted me with big hugs and smiling faces.

"So glad you're home," Dad said with relief in his voice.

"Good to be here," I replied sincerely.

Mom couldn't help commenting on my extensive facial hair. "That's some beard you've got there," she soberly observed. "You aren't planning on keeping it, are you?"

"I honestly don't know," I innocently replied.

"Well, I hope not," Mom said, wishing out loud.

We walked to their car in silence. I opened the car door for Mom to get in the back seat and then got into the front passenger seat.

As Dad drove out of the lot and onto the road leading to the Walt Whitman Bridge, he turned to me and asked in earnest, "So, what are you going to do now?"

Having been away for a whole year without any time to adjust to being home, I had no answer. Extremely disappointed, I wondered if that was the only thing Dad could think about after such a long time apart. We drove the next twenty-five minutes back to my parents' South Jersey apartment in complete silence. My joy quickly turned to sadness, and once again, tears rolled down my face.

But then Rinpoche's perceptive words of wisdom again popped up in the back of my mind. My sadness was a creation of my negative mind. By controlling my mind, I could transform it into positive karma. I began to see my dad's question as a father's valid concern for his son's future. He was deeply worried about me. And honestly, I had some concerns as well. I looked at Dad and said, "You asked what I'm going to do now. I've been thinking a lot about that. It's my top priority, and I'd love to share my thoughts with you."

AFTERWORD

Looking back fifty-two years later, I am forever grateful for having been able to step out of my life in America and embark on my year-long "magical mystery tour." My hungry ghost had a lot to do with it. Never satisfied, he just wouldn't leave me alone until I finally ended up meditating and learning the ways of the Buddha at Kopan. I am in awe of the young spiritual seeker I was then. Traveling halfway around the world alone, I was fearless and open to whatever might come my way.

I'm still a spiritual seeker at heart. Recently, I felt myself more fully embracing an open, allowing energy to guide me, a custom I cultivated during my journey. Though I still put my energy toward achieving a good outcome, I'm feeling the strong pull to be here now, as Ram Dass would say, and allow the natural unfolding of each day. Being consciously present in each moment matters the most to me. Am I in this very moment being compassionate, understanding, supportive, loving, and whatever else increases positive karma in the world today?

My journey, especially the month at Kopan, has had a profound impact on me. The lessons of those travels have stayed with me throughout my life. I know that the willingness to be open, to confront the unknown, and to be my authentic self, as well as my desire to help build a better world, are all lessons I learned during my life-changing odyssey.

I never did make it back to India. Nor did I create the import business I had envisioned back then. What I did do was develop a lasting meditation practice based on the oneness of all existence and the emptiness of all phenomena. I strengthened my practice by attending several retreats at the Insight Meditation Society in Barre, Massachusetts, sitting in sesshins with Zen Master Sasaki Roshi, and maintaining a daily meditation routine. Meditation has helped me develop greater peace of mind by reducing my attachments, desires, and judgments, as well as deepening my belief in the oneness of the universe.

The willingness to be open to what the universe offers me influenced what I would do soon after I returned to the States. A VISTA (Volunteers in Service to America) position at the Western Mass Legal Services office in Greenfield, Massachusetts, unexpectedly fell into my lap. Steven, my former girlfriend France's husband, had just opened a new office there. I spent an evening with them at their home in western Massachusetts not long after arriving back in the States. I found the area where they were living appealing and thought about moving there myself. A few days later, I was back in Jersey at my dad's dental office getting my teeth checked. Out of the blue, Steven called and asked if I wanted a job. The person who was going to take the VISTA position backed out, and he had just twenty-four hours to find a replacement or he would lose the VISTA funding. While I hadn't intended to jump back into practicing law, I felt the universe was sending me a message. How could I refuse?

What I learned at Kopan about our interconnectedness affected other career decisions in my life as well. In the 1980s, I created a nonprofit organization that brought people of different political perspectives together to find common ground and develop a unified approach to peace and security issues. That led to my receiving a US Institute of Peace Fellowship to bring the adversaries in the Nicaraguan civil war together to explore a peaceful resolution to their conflict. Knowing on a deep level that we are all one drew me to this kind of work.

Years later, I founded New Mexicans for Money Out of Politics, which focused on trying to level the playing field for people running for office as well as for those advocating for public policies. That experience resulted in my writing *Breaking Big Money's Grip on America*.

In my personal life, I embraced the concept of oneness by joining several communities bringing people together, including a men's wellness organization, a rural living community, and a spiritual community. I also quickly mended my relationship with my parents as I settled down and got back to practicing law.

At fifty, I became a father. I know my choosing an alternative track in my twenties gave me the insight to allow my daughter to find her own way too. When she went off on a trip abroad by herself right out of high school, I felt she was too young. Still, my year of youthful travel gave me the understanding that this was an invaluable experience that would forever enrich her life. So when she considered coming home early in her travels, I urged her to keep going as I reflected on how important my journey was for me. I was so glad when she decided to resume her worldly exploration.

My hungry ghost has continued to play a significant role in my life as well. When I wasn't satisfied with my life in western Massachusetts, I picked up and moved to New Mexico in 1981. When I felt my law practice was not rewarding, I created nonprofit organizations that met my passion for social change. When my home in Santa Fe no longer suited my needs, I built a home in the country that gratified my desire to be closer to nature. And when my intimate relationships were not fulfilling, I moved on until I found the love of my life.

I am so grateful for my worldly journey that gave me a radically different sense of myself and the world. Being open to what the universe offered me and wherever my travels might take me, I discovered that you don't have to know where you're going to get where you want to be.

Photos from the Author's Journey

Lama Yeshi, head of Kopan monastery.
Photo: Lynda Millspaugh, 1972

Lama Yeshi addressing retreatants in the gompa at Kopan.
Photo: Lynda Millspaugh, 1972

Thubteh Zopa Rinpoche who conducted the meditation retreat.

Bruce Berlin (center) with Lynda Millspaugh (right) and another retreatant during tea break at Kopan monastery.

Bruce Berlin on the throne, pretending to be a groom going to his wedding in Varanasi, India, 1972. Accompanied by friends.

ACKNOWLEDGMENTS

I AM FOREVER INDEBTED TO two Tibetan monks, Lama Yeshe and Thubten Zopa Rinpoche, who taught me the way of the Buddha. Receiving their teachings during a month-long course in Tibetan Buddhism dramatically changed my life. Their joyful presence clearly demonstrated the lofty merit of their chosen path. I am deeply grateful to them for introducing me to how spirit can enhance my life.

I met Lynda Millspaugh during that month. Fifty years later, we reconnected. I very much appreciate her recollections and photos, which aided in my recalling those transcendent times. During my travels, I also received letters from my cousin, Eddie Berlin, my good friend, the late Stan Solomon, and my parents, Dot and Harold Berlin, all of which were very helpful in remembering different phases of my journey.

In writing my memoir, several people read drafts and gave me invaluable feedback. My daughter, Gioia Berlin, reviewed my writing and offered numerous insightful comments, as did her fiancé, Sam Glaser-Nolan. My life partner, Margaret Lubalin, meticulously poured over more than one draft of my memoir, giving me an exceptional critique of each chapter. I also received valuable counsel from my friend Jim Kentch.

For the cover of my book, Joseph Woods provided expert assistance in the design. And finally, I owe my heartfelt gratitude to my editors, Melanie Mulhall and Gina Rae La Cerva, for their insightful work, as well as to Veronica Yager and Cheryl Callighan at Journey Bound Publishing, who turned my story into this book, which I hope will bring back memories of your own inspiring adventures.

ABOUT THE AUTHOR

BRUCE BERLIN HAS BEEN A Buddhist meditator for over fifty years, beginning in the spring of 1973 when he spent a month training with Thubten Zopa Rinpoche and Lama Yeshe at the Kopan monastery outside Kathmandu. Since then, he has attended several sesshins with Zen Master Sasaki Roshi and a number of Vipassana retreats at the Insight Meditation Society in Barre, Massachusetts.

Berlin began his legal career at the Legal Aid Society in Trenton, New Jersey. When he returned from India, he continued his poverty law practice at Western Massachusetts Legal Services in Greenfield, Massachusetts.

Berlin is a former US Institute of Peace Fellow. In 1982, he cofounded and directed New Mexicans for a Bilateral

Nuclear Freeze. He also created and directed The Trinity Forum for International Security and Conflict Resolution to bring together people with diverse political views to find common approaches to such issues as US-Soviet relations and resolving the Nicaraguan War. He later founded and directed New Mexicans for Money Out of Politics.

Prior to his retirement in 2012, he spent eight years as a senior attorney with the New Mexico Public Education Department, where he brought disciplinary charges against educators for violations of the department's code of ethics.

The author of *Breaking Big Money's Grip on America*, Berlin has one daughter and resides in Santa Fe, New Mexico.

www.ingramcontent.com/pod-product-compliance
Lightning Source LLC
Chambersburg PA
CBHW052210090526
44584CB00019BA/2884